Your Personal Guide to Marketing A Nonprofit Organization

Robert S. Topor

Council for Advancement and Support of Education

ISBN 0-89964-254-3

Printed in the United States of America.

In 1974, the American Alumni Council (founded in 1913) and the American College Public Relations Association (founded in 1917) merged to become the Council for Advancement and Support of Education (CASE).

Today, approximately 2,850 colleges, universities, and independent elementary and secondary schools in the U.S. and 23 countries belong to CASE. This makes ours the largest nonprofit 501(c)(3) educational association in terms of institutional membership. Representing the member institutions in CASE are more than 13,000 individual professionals in institutional advancement.

CASE's mission is to advance understanding and support of education for the benefit of society. Central to its mission are its member colleges, universities, and independent schools. CASE fulfills this mission by providing services to beginning, mid-level, and senior advancement professionals; direct services to member institutions; and public affairs programs that bond higher education to the public interest.

CASE offers books, art packages, videotapes, and focus issues of the monthly magazine, CURRENTS, to professionals in institutional advancement. The books cover topics in alumni administration, creative communications, fund raising, government relations, institutional relations, management, marketing, publications, and student recruitment. For a copy of the catalog, RESOURCES, write to the CASE Publications Order Department, 80 South Early Street, Alexandria, VA 22304. For more information about CASE programs and services, call (202) 328-5900.

Book design by Richard Rabil
Cover illustration by Michael David Brown

Council for Advancement and Support of Education
Suite 400, 11 Dupont Circle, Washington, DC 20036

Dedication

O ne of the great joys of working for a nonprofit organization is meeting and getting to know wonderful people. I remember the first time I met Betty. I was employed by Cornell University and was in Chicago to do a speech at a seminar sponsored by the Council for Advancement and Support of Education (CASE). I remember that Betty impressed me. She was a warm, caring, outgoing person. She was one of those people you immediately became attached to. She was fun to be with and a person to cherish as a professional colleague and a personal friend.

Born in Charleroi, Pennsylvania, Betty got her bachelor's degree in journalism from the University of Pittsburgh and her M.A. in communications from Michigan State University.

Although she held a variety of jobs throughout her life, all of them involved marketing and communications, whether she was working in advertising, for a foundation, a research institute, or in her favorite environment—a university. Before coming to the University of Chicago Graduate School of Business where she worked for 10 years as director of publications and public relations, Betty served as editor at Michigan State University and as university editor at Duke University.

Probably one of the best descriptions of Betty appeared in the brochure that was printed for her memorial service on June 4, 1986, in the Joseph Bond Chapel at the University of Chicago.

> She was always curious, always adding to her knowledge and understanding of all the factors that go into the making of a first-class publication—words and pictures, type and paper. But perhaps the best proof of how she used her ability to communicate is the number of friends she made in a lifetime that was not nearly long enough.

Contents

Foreword   i

Preface   iii

Acknowledgements   v

Introduction   vii

Section 1: Understanding Marketing

1. Your Part in the Marketing Process   1

2. What Is Marketing? Why Should You Do It?   7

Section 2: Laying the Groundwork

3. Analyzing Your Organization's Internal Political Environment   13

4. Defining Your Organization's Mission   21

5. Aiming for Target Markets   27

6. Applying Research to Achieve Marketing Results   35

7. Analyzing the Competition   61

8. Trails to Success: Needs Analysis   67

Section 3: The Building Blocks of Marketing

9. Onions, Umbrellas, and Mosaics: Marketing Techniques to Advance Your Organization's Services   71

10. Creating and Executing a Marketing Mix   77

11. Developing a Promotional Plan   83

12. Selecting Promotional Media: A Guide   93

13. Creating Print Advertising   105

14. Using Sales as Part of Your Total Marketing Effort   119

Section 4: The Marketing Planning Map: A Marketing Blueprint

15. Exploring the Marketing Planning Map   125

16. Your Nonprofit Marketing Compass   143

Summary   147

Bibliography   149

About the Author   155

Worksheets and Figures

Worksheets

1. Identify Your Nonprofit Organization's Hierarchy and Internal Political Structure   19

2. Developing Intradisciplinary Marketing Efforts that Cut Across Your Organization's Vertical Boundaries   20

3. Your Nonprofit Organization's Mission Statement   25

4. Target Markets   31

5. Marketing Time-line Monthly Calendar   32

6. Using Target Markets to Achieve Marketing Results   33

7. Determining What Research Needs to be Done   56

8. Demographic Segmentation Variables   58

9. Choosing Your Type of Market Research   60

10. Analyzing Your Competition   65

11. Establishing a Needs Assessment Inventory   70

12. Identifying Your Nonprofit's Services   75

13. A Marketing Plan Outline   80

14. Planning Marketing Action   81

15. Planning and Executing Effective Marketing Promotion   92

16. Planning Promotional Media   102

17. Elements of Print Advertising   116

18. Assessing Your Organization's Current Sales Efforts   123

19. External Forces   140

20. The Four P's of Marketing   141

21. Your Organization's Services   142

Figures

1. The Marketing Process   8

2. Marketing Exchange Process   9

3. A Nonprofit Organization's Internal Political Structure   15

4. Typical Nonprofit Vertical Organizational Structure   18

5. Target Market Acquisition   28

6. Target Market Relationship to Service   29

7. Overlap Potential   29

8. Positioning for a Nonprofit Organization's Services   64

9. Marketing Exchanges Based on Needs Analysis   68

10. Levels of Marketing   72

11. Service Onion   73

12. Integrated Marketing Promotion   86

13. Marketing Planning Map   126

14. Marketing Time-line Monthly Calendar   132

15. Nonprofit Organizational Model   134

16. Your Nonprofit Marketing Compass: Charting Your Course Through the Marketing Planning Map   144

17. Your Completed Nonprofit Marketing Compass   146

Foreword

I am delighted to introduce Bob Topor's latest book on marketing. Bob, whose two previous books for CASE dealt with marketing techniques for educational institutions, now offers his expertise and experience to marketers in the nonprofit sector—those who work for zoos, museums, hospitals, churches and synagogues, symphonies, and social service groups, as well as independent elementary and secondary schools, colleges, and universities.

While marketing has had a relatively long history in business and industry, a marketing approach has come slowly to our organizations, whose financial goals are often as humble as staying in the black. Too often the leaders of nonprofits mistakenly assume that marketing means selling an inferior product at too high a price to people who don't need it.

In *Your Personal Guide to Marketing a Nonprofit Organization*, Bob makes it clear from the start that marketing is not magic. Whatever the business of your nonprofit, if your consumers don't want what you are offering, your organization won't stay in business for long. No matter how slick your promotional material or how clever your slogan, marketing won't sell a bad service or one that no longer meets the needs of its consumers.

We in the nonprofit world may pride ourselves on the very real value of the intangibles we offer—and most of us would be in another line of work if we weren't wholeheartedly enthusiastic about what our particular organization does—but we can no longer afford to stop there. We need marketing if our nonprofits are to continue to play their vital role in today's society.

Competition is as real in the nonprofit sector as it is for the car dealer or the insurance salesman, and we must deal with it. But marketing for nonprofits should not be motivated principally by monetary goals. For the nonprofit marketer, the motivating factor should be the desire to help others by providing them with services that will enrich their lives in some way.

If your organization is to continue to reach its audiences with the services they want and need, you must learn and use the techniques of marketing that Bob sets forth in this guidebook. This involves a complete examination of just what it is you're marketing and to whom.

For example, if your nonprofit organization attracts too few members (or concertgoers or hospital patients or students), you need to look more carefully at your target markets and at your marketing efforts as well as at the services you offer. Perhaps you need to do research on members of your audience. Perhaps you need to schedule your programs or offer your services at a more convenient time and location for the busy working people who might take advantage of them. Or perhaps your promotions are not effective—people won't come to a concert they don't know about; they won't visit a museum they never heard of.

Look at your competition as well. Are you charging a fee for a program the local library offers for free? Is there really a need for this program in your area?

In addition to identifying services that, for one reason or another, no longer appeal to consumers, marketing can also help you identify their need for new services. While no organization should be captive to its consumers and strive in vain to satisfy every whim of an often fickle public, the nonprofit that does not satisfy the needs of its market will not survive.

Marketing helps you cut through clutter and chaos to answer basic questions about your nonprofit organization. Marketing that is based on sound research enables you to see your organization through the eyes of others. In this way, marketing works to destroy false judgments.

Marketing, when it is used in creative and ethical ways, matches the needs of our target audiences with the services our organizations provide and, in so doing, enables your nonprofit to carry out its mission. And that, after all, is our reason for being.

Gary H. Quehl
President, CASE
January 1988

Preface

As is often the case, the student influences and encourages the teacher to reach for new ideas. This guide was written as a result of that kind of creative provocation. In the course of my work for a large nonprofit health care system, Sharp HealthCare in San Diego, I had the privilege of bringing on board a young student intern, Moshe Engelberg. Moshe was working on his master's degree in Public Health, with an emphasis in Health Promotion, at San Diego State University, and he wanted to intern with my organization to gain practical knowledge about marketing and its application to a nonprofit organization. He wanted exposure to an organization that was using marketing to achieve business development goals.

Moshe knew of my work in marketing. He was eager to learn and discuss marketing concepts. He recognized that, for many nonprofit organizations, marketing could make the difference between success and failure, between flourishing and dying.

After many discussions and months of involvement, Moshe challenged me. He said, "What people need is a simple, skills-oriented workbook to show them how to put marketing concepts into action." He went on to describe a book that would explain marketing principles so that they were easy to understand and use. He described a practical guidebook that focused attention on individual skills development, one that would lead the reader through the otherwise complex process of marketing a nonprofit organization.

This guide is the result of Moshe's challenge. I hope you enjoy using it as much as I have enjoyed creating it.

And to Moshe: Thanks for the challenge!

Acknowledgements

Special thanks to Gary H. Quehl, president of the Council for Advancement and Support of Education (CASE), Washington, D.C., for writing the foreword to this book. His enthusiasm and support in publishing this work are greatly appreciated.

A warm and special thanks to Virginia Carter Smith, senior vice president at CASE, for patiently enduring my original manuscript and contributing to improve it. Other "wordspeople" who organized and reorganized to make this book even better were Susan Hunt, CASE's book editor; Julie Landes, CASE's director of marketing and publications; and Carolyn Said, a free-lance editor.

Thanks to the marketing professionals who contributed the sidebars for some of the chapters. Thank you for responding to my request to write up your personal stories. Your information will make this book more useful to the reader.

For allowing me to include his wonderful article, "Let's Take a Survey," and the related "Guidelines for a Mail Survey," a warm handshake to Cletis Pride, vice president of the National Geographic Society in Washington, DC. Also special thanks to Kathleen A. Krentler, associate professor of marketing in the College of Business Administration at San Diego State University, and to William R. Cummins, director of research at Rubin Postaer and Associates, a Los Angeles advertising, public relations, and direct mail marketing firm, for their help with the chapter on market research.

Thanks to my wife Martha and to my sons Mark and Brad, for putting up with my writing at the home computer during odd hours of the night and day, and to our dog Sparkles who did not seem to mind that the printer was running when she was trying to sleep.

But most of all thanks to you, the reader, for your interest in finding ways to help your nonprofit organization market itself. You are the most important person in the whole publishing process. All of our efforts have been dedicated to helping you.

Introduction

Marketing nonprofit organizations is a new idea. Unlike corporate, profit-motivated organizations that have been doing marketing for decades, nonprofits, with their intangible services, have only in the recent past begun to use marketing principles.

The idea of marketing nonprofits can be traced to a book written in 1975 by Philip Kotler, now the Harold T. Martin Professor of Marketing at Northwestern University's J.L. Kellogg Graduate School of Management. With his book, *Marketing for Nonprofit Organizations,* Kotler brought wide attention to the application of marketing concepts to nonprofit organizations. The idea of applying marketing concepts to what are, in most cases, intangible services was a revolutionary one and, needless to say, it was not met with universal acceptance. Most professional organizations were skeptical, not only about using marketing but about the very word itself.

Today, marketing nonprofits is an idea whose time has come. Many factors—chiefly a much more competitive environment—have led nonprofits to consider, and in many cases begin, active marketing programs. Many nonprofit organizations have created new high-level positions for marketers, such as vice president or director of marketing.

This is not to suggest that nonprofits have universally or unequivocally embraced the idea of marketing. Many people and organizations still reject marketing. If your nonprofit organization is one of these, you must introduce the idea cautiously. Even if you think you will have a receptive audience, be prepared to encounter mistrust of marketing as applied to nonprofits. Don't be surprised if you run into resistance!

Becoming an effective marketer

This guide will give you a practical, skills-developing tool to apply marketing concepts and techniques. While marketing can be complex, this guide is intended to be simple in order to encourage the user to apply it in practical ways.

I have written this guide with you, the practitioner, in mind. It is organized by sections. Each section covers important ideas about marketing. Each contributes towards comprehensive marketing. It's your job to study each section, understand its application, network with others in your organization, and apply the ideas to your work. In some cases, application will be obvious. In others, marketing application may require creative efforts on your part. Some sections contain models, checklists, or worksheets to help you. Keep in mind that these are intended only as guides. If they aren't relevant to your situation, don't use them.

I have included, at the end of some chapters, a list of references for further study. Use these to gain more marketing knowledge. I've also included a bibliography at the end of the book.

Implementation: Doing marketing

This guidebook will help you discover the difference between marketing planning, strategy development, and what makes marketing work—implementation. Implementation sets in motion marketing actions that achieve results. Without proper implementation, all the planning and strategy in the world are only an academic exercise.

The following story illustrates this point: The chair of the business department at a prestigious eastern university had a meeting with a corporate official. During the meeting, the corporate official outlined a situation that required marketing assistance for his firm. After carefully listening to the problem presented by the official, the professor said, "I recommend that you hire a couple of my graduate students to help you." After a moment of deliberation, the corporate official said, "No." The professor was surprised. He said, "Why not?" The corporate official shot back, "They couldn't organize a three-car funeral."

Sadly the professor admitted that this was true. In fact, he thought to himself, *he* couldn't solve the problem either. It couldn't be solved by strategy or strategic planning. It required the implementation of marketing ideas to achieve desired results—something neither the graduate students nor the professor could do.

While there are many resources available to help you develop marketing strategy and process, few will help you with marketing implementation. This is because it's easier to write about marketing strategy than to describe implementation, especially good implementation. Planning and strategy can be developed on paper and they can be written about, but implementation means people doing things—people like you.

This guidebook is intended to help you *do* marketing. It will give you the basic tools (knowledge and skills) to implement marketing ideas successfully. It aims to bridge the gap between theory, planning, and strategy development on the one side and action on the other. This guidebook will carry you through the marketing process from research, planning, and strategy development to implementation and evaluation.

One of the most critical factors in effective implementation is attitude. A positive attitude about marketing and its application to nonprofit organizations often spells the difference between failure and success. But keep in mind that marketing is not a panacea. Marketing is not magic. Marketing will not transform poor services to good ones. *Your services must justify the marketing efforts you're planning to expend.* If they don't, your efforts would be better spent on improving your services than on marketing them. The best way to kill a bad product is to market it.

I hope this guidebook will take some of the fear out of marketing your nonprofit organization. The ideas in this guidebook work, but don't blindly accept them as absolute. There are exceptions for every rule and what worked for me may not work for you in exactly the same way. Think about these ideas and methods. Argue about them. Add to them. But *use* them.

Good luck!

Section 1

Understanding Marketing

Chapter 1

Your Part in the Marketing Process

Y*ou* are the most important person in the marketing of your nonprofit organization. Your attitude toward marketing will influence others in your organization. If you are enthusiastic, your enthusiasm will be contagious. And I hope that you will be enthusiastic because you will need enthusiasm to combat the skepticism about marketing that seems to be inherent in most nonprofits.

During my lectures, seminars, and consulting assignments, I am often asked how I became interested in marketing. The answer is always one word: frustration. This frustration had many sources. It included:

- frustration at working in nonprofit organizations and observing how time, effort, people skill, and money are wasted because there is no clear marketing direction;

- frustration at seeing nonprofits "navel-gaze," wasting their valuable resources on looking inward at their own needs, rather than focusing on critical external audiences—this is "inside-out" thinking rather than "outside-in";

- frustration at observing how poorly nonprofits treat their target audiences as a consequence of their inside-out viewpoint;

- frustration at seeing one part of a nonprofit organization advance itself at the expense of another part or at the expense of the parent organization (I call this "self-destruction through fragmentation");

- frustration at talking with key administrators who think marketing is *only* promotion and fail to realize that true nonprofit marketing is a process, an activity that, when well executed, becomes a pervasive—and positive—force throughout an organization;

- frustration at talking with presidents, administrators, CEOs, and board members who think marketing should be anathema to nonprofits; "We're good," is their attitude, "and we will flourish because we're good. We don't need marketing for our organization"; and, finally,

- frustration because some people are afraid of new ideas, new concepts, and

1

new beginnings. They're set in their ways. They're unwilling to give up their complacency to risk marketing.

Defining marketing

What is marketing that it should meet with so much resistance on the part of those who need it so much? I define marketing as the analysis, planning, and implementation of programs designed to bring about desired exchanges with designated markets. These exchanges are directed at target markets (groups of pre-identified people) for the purpose of achieving the organization's goals. Marketing relies heavily on the organization's ability to prepare and present its products, offerings, or services so that they answer the needs and wants of these target markets.

Marketing has several stages:
- product understanding—analyzing your organization's services;
- pricing—realizing that everything, even someone's time, has a price;
- distribution—using the best methods to get your organization's services to target markets; and
- communication—communicating your services in terms of the wants and needs of your target markets. Sales should also be included here; your approach to sales will be quite different from that of the hard-product, profit-motivated marketer.

We can also look at marketing in terms of the 4 P's—the basic ideas of marketing. **P**roduct is the service offered by your nonprofit. **P**lace is the location(s) where users can get your services. **P**rice is what the user "pays" to get your product or service. (Remember that for nonprofits price can be monetary or abstract—a user may give up time to take advantage of your service.) **P**romotion is the activity created to communicate your service to your target market(s).

This long description of marketing shows you that marketing is not a single, isolated activity; it's a process.

Marketing skills

To become an effective nonprofit marketer, you need to develop two kinds of skills, which I classify under the headings *art* and *science*. Marketing arts include skills such as writing, design, typography, visualization, communications concept development, promotion, advertising, public relations, community event planning, creative strategy planning, and distribution.

Under the science heading I include such marketing skills as research planning, surveying, demographic analysis, budgetary planning, business development, return-on-investment analysis, evaluative research, and strategic analysis.

Don't be frightened by these categories of skills. Chances are you feel that your strengths lie in one category or the other; few people are confident of their skills in both categories. But you will develop the skills you don't have or you will identify other people—either in-house or outside—who can help you in your weak areas. Effective marketing is *not* a solo activity; it's a team process.

This guidebook is not intended to be the only marketing tool you will need. It's intended to whet your appetite for marketing. It will give you marketing ideas that you can put to use. You can use this guide to encourage others to participate. And most of all, I hope it will convince you that *you* are the most important person in marketing your nonprofit organization.

For further reading

Some excellent resources to help you apply marketing ideas to your nonprofit organization include:

Brandt, Steven C. *Entrepreneuring: The 10 Commandments for Building a Growth Company.* New York: New American Library, 1982.

Drucker, Peter F. *Managing for Results.* New York: Harper & Row, 1964.

Kotler, Philip. *Marketing for Nonprofit Organizations.* Englewood Cliffs, NJ: Prentice-Hall, 1975; revised 1982.

Kotler, Philip, et al. *Cases and Readings for Marketing for Nonprofit Organizations.* Englewood Cliffs, NJ: Prentice-Hall, 1983.

Levitt, Theodore. *The Marketing Imagination.* New York: The Free Press, 1983.

McCormack, Mark H. *What They Don't Teach You at Harvard Business School.* New York: Bantam Books, 1984.

Naisbitt, John. *Megatrends.* New York: Warner Books, 1984.

Peters, Thomas J., and Waterman, Robert H., Jr. *In Search of Excellence.* New York: Warner Books, 1982.

Ray, Michael, and Myers, Rochelle. *Creativity in Business.* Garden City, NY: Doubleday, 1986. An excellent and highly enjoyable book, based on the famous Stanford University course that has revolutionized the art of business success.

Carole Towne, director of public relations and marketing at the San Diego Zoo, has a passion not only for marketing but also for the "product" she markets—the protection of wildlife and the education of the visiting public.

Meet the Needs of Your Public

At the San Diego Zoo we are fortunate to have a long tradition of being oriented to marketing. Unlike most other zoos, which have been tax-supported, throughout the San Diego Zoo's history it has been dependent on the income it generates—through admissions fees, membership dues, donations, and the sale of tours, gifts, and food. Thus in the present climate, when tax support for many public institutions is disappearing, the San Diego Zoo has a head start over other zoos, which have only recently had to find new ways to fund their operations.

At the same time zoos everywhere are struggling to find new sources of income, they are facing a larger test. Dramatically increased pressures on the earth's wild spaces, and therefore on its wildlife inhabitants, mean that for many animal species zoos offer a last chance for survival. Zoos have taken on the challenge of the preservation of many of these endangered species.

The challenge is immense. Zoos face a tremendous task in attempting to assure the long-term survival of rare animals that may have no other home. The enormity of the task can cause us temporarily to lose sight of our other obligations.

So at times, we must remind ourselves of the needs of those for whom we hold our animals in trust—our visitors. The very definition of "zoo" includes the visiting public. We must constantly strive to maintain a balance that allows us to meet the needs of both the precious animals entrusted to us and of the visiting public that makes our ambitious programs possible. For without such a balance, zoos themselves will not survive.

Joan Trezek, formerly vice president of public affairs and marketing for John Muir Hospital in Walnut Creek, California, shares Towne's enthusiasm for marketing.

Listen to Your Customers

To be a marketing-driven organization represents a marked change from the way most not-for-profits operate. Until recently most health care and educational institutions decided what services they were going to provide and in what context and said, in effect, "Come and get it." That's a kind of paternalistic "Father knows best" approach.

The people who know best are the customers our organizations seek to serve—they are the ones whose wants and needs should call the shots. And half the fun of marketing is getting to know the customer. Have fun—and listen up!

Lynne Cunningham is the principal of Cunningham Associates, a marketing research and planning firm in Sacramento, California, that specializes in the health care industry.

Think Strawberries

I would be remiss if I didn't encourage your readers to "think strawberries." The strawberry that has become my logo and synonymous with the Cunningham Associates' commitment to marketing goes back many years to a speech by Jim Lavenson, the manager of the Plaza Hotel in New York. Lavenson's theory was that every employee should be a marketing representative for the Plaza. To achieve his marketing goals, he implemented programs that allowed employees to spend a night in the hotel as part of their orientation and specifically required entertainers to perform in the employee cafeteria before performing in the fancy hotel lounge.

The waiters in the fancy restaurant at the Plaza got hooked on the program when Lavenson started flying in fresh strawberries for the dessert cart. Even patrons on diets would choose fresh strawberries for dessert. The bills went up, the tips went up, and the waiters were hooked on the program, which became known as "Think Strawberries." Lavenson's message and the theme that I have adopted is that our internal audiences are key to the success of any marketing program.

Lavenson's strawberry theory is consistent with the "management by wandering around" concept of Tom Peters (co-author of *In Search of Excellence* and *A Passion for Excellence*). The commitment to thinking strawberries or to marketing must start at the top of the organization with a commitment to be aware of what's going on, and to be proud of an organization and really "sell" it to its various publics. As a consultant, I see far too many nonprofits spending thousands of dollars on advertising only to have the product "demarketed" or "unsold" by employees who are not part of the program or are not in tune with the organization's goals.

So, I guess the first attitude that has contributed to my "marketing success" is "thinking strawberries."

Chapter 2

What Is Marketing?
Why Should You Do It?

Unfortunately, marketing as it relates to nonprofit organizations is often badly misunderstood. Most people think only of promotion. They think of advertising, news releases, and logos. While this guidebook does cover promotion, promotion is only a small part of the marketing process. Many steps must take place in your marketing effort before you are ready to begin promotion.

Most people think of its negative aspects when they think of marketing. They think of selling poor products or of manipulating unsuspecting consumers, often with intent to deceive. Marketing can be—and all too often is—misused. But this guidebook demonstrates how marketing, when you use it in ethical and creative ways, can be a powerful force in helping your nonprofit organization meet challenges and achieve goals.

What is marketing?

The simplest way to describe marketing is by calling it an exchange process: Someone gives something in exchange for something else. For example, the patron of a symphony orchestra gives up time and money to attend a concert. Someone else gives time and money to attend an educational seminar sponsored by your organization. This concept of exchange—giving one thing for another—is central to the definition of marketing.

Marketing is a process, not a one-time, isolated activity. Marketing is a continuum of efforts—researched, planned, executed, and evaluated to achieve organizational goals and objectives. Marketing occurs over time; it is cyclical. While marketing has a beginning, it should have no end but start over again, as in Figure 1.

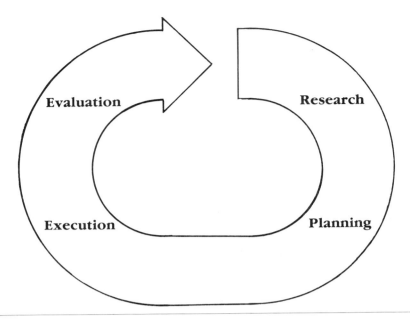

Figure 1: The Marketing Process

You can think of the marketing process in relation to many organizational levels. You can market a product, many products, collections of products (product mixes), or your whole organization. (When I say "product" here, I mean the product, service, or offering of a nonprofit organization. In this guidebook, for the sake of simplicity, I'll refer to your organization's products, services, or offerings as "services." The services of a symphony orchestra are its concerts; a museum's services are its exhibits; a health care organization's its medical services.)

A large nonprofit organization such as a university can market a course, many courses (a major), or collections of courses (departments or colleges). It can market the whole university, or it can market by activities (sports, music, public lectures, community relations) or by audiences (students, faculty, parents, alumni). You can see that there are many different ways to market a nonprofit organization.

Why use marketing?

Why should a nonprofit organization use marketing? Probably the best way to answer this question is to describe what happens when an organization *doesn't* use marketing. For many years I worked as an assistant administrator at a university in upstate New York. The institution had no interest in using marketing to advance itself. I found many of the attitudes typical of nonprofit organizations: "We're good, we don't need to market ourselves." "If people want our services, they will seek us out." And "Marketing is a nasty activity. It's like selling toothpaste—it's not for us. We're above that."

Many of these negative ideas came crashing in on me one morning. As often was the case, I arrived at work early but, much to my surprise, I found that the lobby and hallway of the administration building were crowded with students. Some were asleep on the floor. As I tiptoed carefully over the bodies, I asked a student why everyone was there. He responded, "Oh, this is part of our registration process. If we don't get here by 5 a.m., we have to stand in line all day, and all the good courses are filled. When I got to my office, I sat down at my desk and thought about my own college days. No one had to get up at 5 in the morning to register. Registration was computerized. And my alma mater was a much larger institution with thousands more students.

I thought about all those people out there in the hallway. How would they feel about this institution after they graduated and began receiving frequent appeals for donations? How would they feel about their alma mater when their children were ready to select a college or university? What feelings would they have when the alumni office sent a letter to enlist their support? What would they tell friends about their college experience?

That university was doing a poor job of marketing to its most important target market audience—its students. And this was not an isolated incident. It was indicative of a pervasive attitude. I remember that some faculty and administrators would say, "This would be a nice place to work if there were no students here." No students! Without students there would be no reason for higher education, let alone this particular university. Many people who have worked for a nonprofit are all too familiar with this attitude and the problems that result from it.

An organization with a good marketing program will never forget the importance of its "customers" in this way. For marketing is the process that examines *both* sides of the exchange illustrated in Figure 2, not just the organization's.

Figure 2: Marketing Exchange Process

In some ways, marketing is just common sense. But marketing also involves sophisticated techniques and methods. The health care industry provides an excellent example of successful marketing. Hospitals have traditionally taken a passive "We're here—they will come to us" attitude, typical of many nonprofit organizations. But more recently, many hospitals have begun to apply marketing concepts to achieve business development goals.

How are they doing this? First, they have accepted the fact that it's no longer business as usual. Pressures (environmental, technological, political, competitive, economic, and societal) have forced them to adopt new ways of thinking about health care.

These progressive health care organizations have organized their services by "product lines." This system of marketing is based on an analysis of consumer (physician, patient, third-party payor) wants and needs. These health care institutions organize and deliver services that are based on need analysis. For example, for many decades the typical birthing environment was a sterile hospital delivery room. Research of consumer wants and needs has led many health care institutions to develop alternate birthing environments. These environments are not the typical white, equipment-saturated operating rooms. They more closely resemble a home environment—a comfortable room with many amenities that appeal to the mother, her new baby, friends, and family.

The result of such need analysis is "proactive marketing." Proactive marketing uses techniques to *anticipate* user wants and needs. Proactive marketing puts focus on external target markets in order to plan, deliver, evaluate, and improve services. The users benefit from better services and quicker responses to needs, and the nonprofit organization benefits from stronger business development.

It's a joy to find a nonprofit organization that applies marketing concepts effectively by combining them with other efforts such as strategic planning and implementation through public relations and other efforts. Many nonprofits have difficulty orienting their efforts to "bridge" their internal concerns and important external audiences. A nonprofit organization that has been successful in bridging the gap between services and external users and audiences is Carnegie Mellon University. R. Keith Moore, vice president for university relations, describes the importance of marketing in helping his office help the university.

The Marketing Bridge

Our media visibility efforts concentrate on the national news media, and we have enjoyed some success in spreading the university's recruiting base from 50 percent inside the commonwealth of Pennsylvania to 72 percent outside the commonwealth, in less than six years. One of the primary mistakes a press officer makes is to direct attempts to attract news coverage to only those newspapers that will respond easily. Instead, you must direct your efforts to obtain coverage to the most cost-effective ways. We spend an hour trying to place a story in the *New York Times* with a circulation of 1.5 million readers rather than an hour approaching an editor of a smaller newspaper with a circulation of under 50,000 readers. While we will not hit as often in the *New York Times* as we will in the small newspaper, we still come out well ahead because our placement reaches far more people.

On a related but different front, as we practice marketing at Carnegie Mellon, it involves looking at the marketplace and bringing our product closer to what the market needs. Our marketplace, education, gives dramatic signs of what society needs most. And without sacrificing the integrity of the institution's educational mission, we periodically (every three or four years) hold strategic planning sessions with the faculty and administration to modify existing programs to come in line with society's needs.

Since our promotion efforts continue to bring more applications from better students, attract higher quality faculty than in the past, gain increases in private and government support, and build respect among alumni in the field, we believe strongly that strategic planning applied with marketing principles is the way to go. This strategic plan then drives everything my public relations operation does in support of the goals of the plan.

Unfortunately, only a handful of academic institutions engage in putting together a market-based strategic plan. The plans of most institutions are often based on internal considerations such as which departments have faculty who are retiring, which classrooms have surplus space, which computer company can provide free equipment, and other considerations that merely muddle their "grand vision" for their institution. These muddlings, though often imperative for operating the enterprise, obscure pertinent factors from the society's marketplace.

The successful nonprofit marketer recognizes that the integration of traditional functions and activities (publicity through news placement, public relations, community affairs, advertising and promotion, development, special events, and fund raising, etc.) to achieve organizational goals can be very powerful. Marketing is a force that, when combined with other forces, can achieve dramatic results.

Unfortunately, for many nonprofit organizations, marketing is often perceived as a threat to existing functions. One of your greatest challenges is to find ways to introduce marketing and to get your organization to accept it.

There is no surefire way to do this. It depends, to a great degree, on the nonprofit organization itself and the people involved in that organization. Chapter 3, "Analyzing Your Organization's Internal Political Environment," is designed to help you understand your organization so that you can determine how to proceed. It will help you discover how to introduce marketing concepts, how to get your nonprofit to embrace and execute effective marketing, and how to get results.

Section 2

Laying the Groundwork

Chapter 3

Analyzing Your Organization's Internal Political Environment

For many years I was employed by a university in upstate New York. One day a friend who worked for Eastman Kodak Company said to me, "It must be wonderful to work for a university. You don't have any of the political problems we have at Kodak." It was obvious to me—and it probably is to you too—that my friend had never been employed by a nonprofit organization. Otherwise she would have known that nonprofits are certainly as political—if not more political—than most profit-motivated corporations. And marketing has a great deal to do with the internal politics and political pressures of the organization.

If you want to be a successful marketer, you must begin by studying your political environment. If your organization's political waters run deep, this may not be easy. Who holds the keys to power? Where are decisions made? Who influences whom and why? Who holds fiscal control?

Because a nonprofit organization is usually an organization with an altruistic mission, its primary motive is not profit. In most cases, however, it is concerned about income generation (if only to cover costs) as well as return on investment. It is rare to find a nonprofit organization that is not interested in the bottom line.

The obvious difference between a for-profit organization and a nonprofit organization is the fact that someone (owners, partners, corporate stockholders) benefits financially from the success of a profit-making organization. Motivating factors for a nonprofit organization are much more altruistic: Most nonprofits exist to deliver a benefit or service to their users. Related to these different motivational factors are issues of taxation. Because the nonprofit organization is not driven by profit making, it enjoys distinct local, state, and federal tax advantages.

Nonprofits are diverse: zoos; museums; hospitals; independent schools, colleges, and universities; foundations; charitable organizations; churches; government agencies; political groups; social action groups; symphonies; libraries; and so on. Despite differences in mission, nonprofits have one common denominator: They are hierarchies. They have structure. They are political. But this political force is not one of the external political forces you might normally think about—that is, those involved in the perennial struggle between the donkeys and the elephants. This is an *internal* political force.

Internal political forces can take two forms, positional and personal. Positional political power results from a person's level in the organizational structure. The higher up the ladder, the more political power the person in that position holds— the CEO usually has the most positional power.

Personal political power results from qualities possessed by the individual. Certain people possess power that results from character, demeanor, experience, or how they are viewed by others. Personal power is usually harder to predict than positional power. You can identify positional power by studying your nonprofit's organization charts, but personal power is the result of relationships that are much more difficult to identify. Nevertheless, you must consider both forms of political power. Internal political forces in nonprofit organizations are often direct reflections of their hierarchical structure. Figure 3 illustrates the hierarchy for most nonprofit organizations.

You can see that many pressures are at work in this important diagram. As the arrows show, these pressures (political forces) operate from top to bottom. Let's begin at the top. Nonprofit organizations are under political pressure from the general public. Unlike profit-motivated corporations that may be concerned about stockholders or other distinct pressure groups, most nonprofits must answer to a wider public.

Political pressures from this public are focused on a board of directors or a group of trustees. Ostensibly this leadership group guides the nonprofit organization; however, the leadership group is designed to represent the general public. Therefore the board of trustees or directors has two strong interests—internal and external. The board is the bridge between the general public and the nonprofit organization, and it responds to pressures from both directions. It's important to remember this when you are planning your marketing efforts. In many ways your directors or trustees act as antennae to measure and respond to political pressures from the general public. At the same time, they may respond to key individuals within your organization.

These pressures can take many forms. Some can be overt such as pressure from a board member to take an action that will affect your organization. Others can be subtle—nuances, feelings, or ideas that find their way down the hierarchical structure. For example, a board member can put pressure on your organization's chief executive officer about one of your nonprofit's offerings because a friend or relative didn't like it. You may feel this pressure or might receive a request without any explanation of what really happened. The better you are able to un-

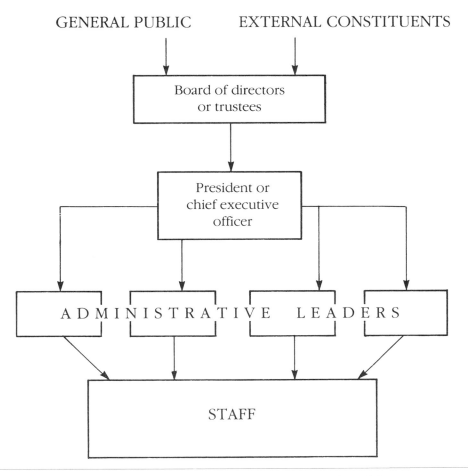

Figure 3: A Nonprofit Organization's Internal Political Structure

derstand these subtle pressures, and where they come from, the more successful you will be at dealing with them.

You will find that you will be able to use marketing concepts to avoid and respond to these political pressures. You can also help your president or CEO respond to pressures from your board by keeping him or her supplied with marketing information.

Your president or chief executive officer is the focal point for pressures at the top. He or she receives direction from the leadership board and, in turn, redirects that pressure into the proper channels in the organization, usually through administrative leaders. Depending on the size of your nonprofit organization, these leaders could be one or two people or a staff of vice presidents. In a nonprofit organization, political pressures can be great at this point because the president and the administrators are usually concerned about doing what is perceived as necessary—that is, following directions of the leadership at the highest levels in the organizational structure. Administrative leaders then turn to staff to execute and carry out directions from above.

It's important to understand these pressures before you begin your efforts to market or to introduce marketing to your organization. Some people may interpret your efforts to introduce marketing as an attempt to gain power (budgetary, personnel, or material) or to advance your own position in the organization.

Before marketing is introduced to your nonprofit organization, therefore, you must consider how it will be received, supported, or rejected at various levels in the organizational hierarchy. One of the first questions to ask yourself is, Who will introduce marketing? You? A consultant? A marketing committee? Can it most successfully be introduced at the top (board level)? Or should it begin as a grass-roots activity (at the staff level)? Should both methods be used? How should it be introduced? As an educational process? These are important questions, and the ultimate success of your organization's marketing plan will depend on how wisely they have been answered.

I knew a nonprofit organization that hired a director of marketing without considering these questions and without assessing internal political pressures. This unfortunate person received very little support and met resistance at every organizational level. He was not wise enough—or skillful enough—to overcome the pressures he faced, and he failed. Attempts to introduce marketing were set aside, much to the detriment of the organization.

Before introducing marketing to your nonprofit organization, you will need to analyze internal political pressures. Use Worksheet 1 at the end of this chapter to identify pivotal people at all levels of your organization on whose support you can count. Motives are important. Consider why each key person has a vested interest in the outcomes that marketing could provide. Relate marketing concepts to how marketing can best serve these vested interests.

Many organizations, in their effort to embrace marketing, are confused about where to put it in the organizational structure. Some nonprofits mistakenly believe that marketing is a new addition, rather than a process that relates to the whole organization. Some nonprofits are further confused by the fact that many existing activities (public relations, public affairs, development, institutional advancement, community relations) already embrace marketing and claim it as their responsibility. This is unfortunate, and it shows that marketing is badly misunderstood. Marketing is not an isolated add-on, but a pervasive process affecting every part of a nonprofit's activities. To succeed, all current activities must accept and incorporate marketing.

Further, a nonprofit cannot consider marketing to be the responsibility of one person. Although an organization can hire people with marketing expertise and responsibility, marketing will not result from this action alone, any more than a thorough business plan will instantly appear when an accountant is hired. It takes the whole organization to implement marketing.

The question of where to put marketing in a nonprofit organization has a simple answer: everywhere.

To be pervasive and effective, however, marketing must have its champions. Nonprofit organizations should consider hiring a vice president for marketing. The position should be high enough in the organizational structure to cut across traditional vertical organizational boundaries. It should be equivalent in power to that of other organizational unit leaders. The marketing leader must have the power to effect changes as necessary.

You will find that some people react negatively to the language of marketing. Even the word "marketing" often raises hackles. Other words that are "dangerous" are "product," "advertising," "selling," and "promotion." You can avoid this problem by using words that are more "comfortable" to describe marketing concepts. For instance, instead of marketing, use "institutional advancement," "public affairs," "public relations," "community affairs," or some other euphemism. For "products," use "services." You will find that you can achieve the same marketing objectives without turning off some of the key people with whom you must work. Remember that it's not the words that are important but the concepts. Use marketing concepts to introduce marketing concepts.

Another aspect of the nonprofit organization that may present a problem in your attempts to develop collective, organization-wide marketing is its vertical organization (Figure 4 on the next page). The typical nonprofit organization is made up of vertical components—departments, units, or sets of activities—which, in most cases, have their own organizational structure, their own administrative leaders, functions, and, in some cases, mission. Each unit offers services to the marketplace. Although the units are organized under the umbrella of the nonprofit organization, they often operate with great autonomy.

In the past, when nonprofits were driven by their internal needs and did not have to pay much attention to their external markets, this autonomy presented no problem. But for a contemporary, market-sensitive, externally driven organization, the autonomous vertical-unit organization can create great difficulties. In many cases, this kind of organization does not allow quick and easy development of intradisciplinary services, nor does it encourage promotion across vertical lines. Instead, it is more likely to lead to competition of organizational subunits, often at the expense of the collective parent organization.

One way to deal with the marketing problems created by this organizational structure is to market your services by product line. In many cases these product lines will cross traditional organizational boundaries. You might consider creating a product line team, a group of people drawn from each organizational unit. To broaden the group you might include other representatives as well. The objective is to create a team that will be able to market your services from the users' viewpoint. This is also an excellent way to get cooperation from sections of your organization that would not normally work well together.

For example, a university might discover through research an opportunity to create a new division of summer sessions. It may have found evidence of the need for summertime education or identified a potential market for it. Traditionally, a university comprises many colleges: each college has departments, and each department is headed by a dean. The new summer session curriculum would include courses from many departments. Thus, this new product line, summer ses-

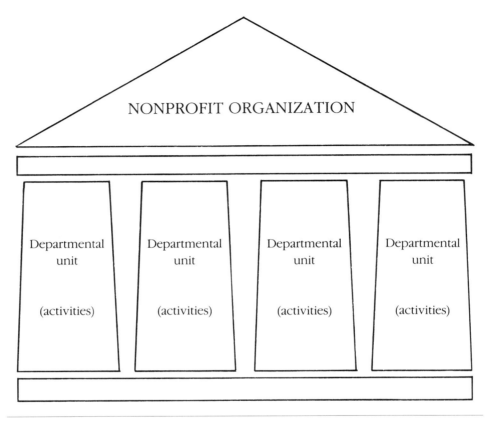

Figure 4: Typical Nonprofit Vertical Organizational Structure

sions, would cross traditional vertical boundaries (colleges and departments).

A marketing team, composed of members from each college, would be most effective in creating this new product line.

By approaching this problem from the consumers' point of view, rather than the organization's, you will be able to cross traditional vertical boundaries. Use research to support your efforts. Use research to develop services that respond to consumers' needs. Seize every opportunity to eliminate vertical barriers, but do it carefully. You will probably be breaking new ground.

Worksheet 2 at the end of this chapter can help you develop intradisciplinary marketing efforts. Use this worksheet to identify services provided by your organization that are good candidates for intradisciplinary marketing that cuts across vertical boundaries.

Worksheet 1

Identify Your Nonprofit Organization's
Hierarchy and Internal Political Structure

> Board of directors or trustees

> President or chief executive officer

> Administrative leaders

> Staff

In each box, list the names (or initials) of key individuals at each level of your organization. Put an asterisk (*) next to the name of each individual with personal power. Put two asterisks (**) next to those people who will support marketing concepts. Decide how to introduce marketing at each level of your organization.

Worksheet 2

Developing Intradisciplinary Marketing Efforts
That Cut Across Your Organization's Vertical Boundaries

Service	Originating department	Possible intradisciplinary collective marketing	Name

1. List your organization's services.

2. Identify originating department for each service.

3. Put an X in the collective marketing column to suggest which services might be offered as intradisciplinary collective packages to the marketplace.

4. In the right-hand column suggest a name or title for the collective package.

Chapter 4

Defining Your Organization's Mission

Mission. Let's think about that word and the images it brings to mind. You might think of the Crusaders, bands of people driven by religious fervor, traveling to distant destinations under banners that proclaimed their allegiance. Or you might think of a John Wayne movie: World War II, a military mission, Marines fighting their way through a remote Pacific island jungle. Or you might think of a NASA mission: an outer-space exploration designed to accomplish some interstellar objective. Now think of yourself, the nonprofit marketer, as a modern-day missionary, a person dedicated to carrying out the mission of your particular organization.

Most nonprofit organizations had a clear mission when they were founded. If you dig deep enough into the historical archives of your nonprofit, you will probably find a statement describing its mission—its reason for being, its vision of the future, its major goals and philosophy, its commitments and dedications.

Why is a mission statement important?

A nonprofit organization is a complex political organization composed of many components and pressured by many forces, internal and external. It needs direction and focus. A mission statement is a written description of purpose that can be used to research, plan, develop, execute, and monitor the nonprofit's programs. A good, up-to-date mission statement can be the yardstick against which marketing efforts are measured, the divining rod used to develop new ventures, and a balance against which to weigh new programs.

A word of caution: Many nonprofit organizations have written mission statements that can best be described as "high-falutin." These are obscure philosophical statements that have little or no value from a marketing point of view. They cannot be used to position the organization among competitors or to relate services to the parent organization. Nor are these mission statements accurate enough to help guide marketing and promotional strategy development by identifying needs and wants of target audiences. The mission statement, to have marketing usefulness, must be concise, accurate, focused, and precise.

Take a little time to look for your organization's mission statement. When you find one, ask yourself if it is accurate, up-to-date, concise, and usable. Will it help you achieve marketing objectives? Don't be surprised if there is no mission statement in printed form. If the mission is not written out per se, look for statements of organizational purpose in speeches, promotional materials, annual reports, and other documents. Use clues from these materials and what you know of your organization's reason for being to create a draft mission statement.

As you develop an accurate, marketing-related mission statement, consider your organization's scope—the target markets for its services. Think of the people your organization serves.

Values make up another element of your organization's mission. Your organization's values are important guiding principles; they may include quality, honesty, trust, service, caring, meticulousness, and dedication. If you can describe these abstract ideas in concrete terms in the mission statement, you can use them later to develop promotional and advertising strategies.

Your nonprofit organization's mission statement should include:

• identification of primary, secondary, and tertiary target markets (users of your nonprofit's services);

• key words that describe the values that are important to your organization;

• a brief description of your nonprofit's history, but be sure to include present-day information; tie today's services to yesterday's history;

• "blue-skying"—where is your organization headed? Why? What new ideas, concepts, and technologies will it use to shape itself in the future?

• people—who are the people that are leading your organization? How do their philosophies and interests shape your nonprofit's services?

• a clear description of the business of your organization—what it really does;

• objectives—what variables will your nonprofit emphasize (market share, profitability, reputation); and

• goals—your nonprofit's specific objectives with respect to scope, time, and who is responsible.

Use Worksheet 3 to develop a mission statement for your organization.

CASE's Mission Statement

The Council for Advancement and Support of Education advances understanding and support of education for the benefit of society. We fulfill this mission by providing (1) services to beginning, mid-level, and senior professionals; (2) direct services to institutions; and (3) public affairs programs that bond higher education to the public interest.

Writing in the September 1982 CASE CURRENTS, *Carol J. Guardo (then provost of the University of Hartford and now president of Rhode Island College) outlined the elements of a mission statement. Whether you work for a college, university, independent school, zoo, museum, civic organization, health care service, church or synagogue, credit union, political organization, or condominium management team, the following excerpt from her article will be helpful in describing how a non-profit mission statement is prepared. Note that the headings form an outline that can be applied to any nonprofit organization. Use them to help define your institution's mission.*

Defining the Mission of a University

In the best of worlds, the academic mission, image, and marketing approach of a university are logically and inextricably integrated. However, this ideal is seldom realized.

As many as half-a-dozen different departments may have responsibility for handling various aspects of mission and marketing. It takes a concerted effort by the academic and promotional arms of the institution if they are to work together in a mutually supportive way.

Substance

A university's mission statement sums up the academic identity of the institution. It covers the type of educational institution the university is, the kind of educational philosophy it espouses, and the specific educational aims and purposes it seeks to fulfill.

The goal is clear—a mission statement and a sense of mission that are explicit and coherent. To achieve this requires a systematic process where all constituencies identify and accept the academic mission of a university.

One approach to the task involves a process of self-examination organized around three basic questions:
- What is the current operational definition of the institution?
- At what point in its history or development does it find itself?
- What kind of educational institution is this particular university?

A. Define the institution

For an operational definition of a university, look at its curricula. Curricula translate educational philosophy into actual teaching/learning experiences. Study them to gain insights into the kinds and purposes of education that your institution currently serves.

Also, identify the kinds and levels of programs being offered to students. For example, you may find that programs are primarily undergraduate or graduate, in liberal arts or professional studies. Students may be primarily full-time or part-time, residential or commuting, traditional

18- to 22-year-olds or older adults.

Be sure to note how well the design characteristics of the curricula fit the actual characteristics of the students. The poorer the fit, the less likely it is that the university is fulfilling its stated mission. A poor fit also raises questions about how the institution is portraying itself and marketing its programs.

You should also decide whether or not the university plans to continue offering the same kinds and levels of programs in the future. And will it be serving the same student clientele? Is change necessary or only desirable? Is change feasible? Or might the institution be better served by continuing its present course and mission?

B. Determine the historic moment

A second step in identifying the substance of a university's mission involves determining its historic moment. At what point in its history or development does your institution stand? Is it in an early phase of development or in its maturity?

You will encounter problems if the institution is being portrayed or marketed at variance with its developmental phase. For example, trying to convey a sense of tradition for a relatively young institution can be fruitless. Equally fruitless is trying to convey a sense of dynamic expansion during a period of consolidation.

C. Categorize the institution

The third question you must ask relates to the kind of educational institution the university is. In this regard, the Carnegie Commission categories can be a useful starting point. [Carnegie categories include research, doctoral, and comprehensive universities; selective liberal arts, liberal arts, and two-year colleges.] It categorizes each institution in terms of academic, fiscal, and student characteristics.

Studying the features and indices of other institutions like yours will help you achieve a more accurate identity. Then your college or university won't promote itself as parochial when its curriculum is secular, claim to be a liberal arts institution when it is really engaged in professional education, or advertise its commitment to teaching when most senior professors are engaged only in research. Here you need to distinguish between appearance and reality, between what was and what is, between what an institution hopes to be and what it can be.

False images create problems. They give rise to dissonance and disappointment both within and outside the university. They cause disjunctions between mission and market. On the other hand, explicit, coherent mission statements foster the integration of mission, market, and image.

Worksheet 3

Your Nonprofit Organization's Mission Statement

\

\

\

\

\

\

\

\
---

1. List the ideas that describe your organization's mission.

2. Edit, refine, and distill these ideas to create a concise statement that best describes your organization's mission.

3. Think about how you would write your organization's mission statement from the points of view of your many target audiences. Consolidate those ideas.

4. Circulate your mission statement draft to many people inside and outside your organization. Get reactions. Measure those carefully against reality and your organization's services to see if these services are accomplishing your described mission.

5. When the final version of your mission statement is ready, you may want to get it typeset and printed so that you can distribute it throughout your organization. Make it a key part of your marketing efforts. Put a framed copy in your office. Think about it frequently.

6. You will know if your organization's mission statement is valid if you can see the impact it has on the organization's services, and if you can see it in much of the promotional material—printed materials, speeches, advertising, and promotion—used to advance your organization and its services.

Chapter 5

Aiming for Target Markets

L et's consider how you will identify target markets, groups of people who are currently or potentially important to your organization. You may want to identify market segments (subdivisions of your market) by demographic, geographic, psychographic, or behavioral characteristics. You may think of other criteria that relate to your organization's mission and services.

Be broad in your thinking. Think of target markets represented by funding sources, subcontract customers, prospective direct and indirect referral sources, and any other potential users.

For example, a liberal arts college located in a suburban area might, for admissions purposes, define several discrete target markets: high school students interested in advanced study in liberal arts, high school counselors, parents, high school friends of current college students (peer influence), the local Rotary Club (may sponsor a scholarship for liberal arts study), local businesses (may participate in a cooperative study program for liberal arts students), media people (newspaper editors may be persuaded to write about the value of liberal arts in today's business world), alumni (may help identify potential students), community leaders, and clubs or organizations that are representative of the college's interest in liberal arts and may be in a position to influence an admissions decision.

A key idea in target marketing is behavior. Ask yourself how each market segment will react to your services. Will these people be receptive or resistant? To answer this, you need to do research to determine their attitudes, perceptions, values, personalities, learning style, family roles, social class, income, subculture, and so on. (Chapter 6 will help you do that.)

You must decide which market segments you will approach through direct actions, such as promotional campaigns aimed at distinct audiences, and which will require an indirect approach through a third party (see Figure 5 on the next page). For example, a health care organization may direct marketing efforts toward a corporate contractor (a third party) in order to get health care patient referrals. A community college may contract with a local manufacturer to bring classes for foremen or machine operators into the factory. These are examples of indirect target market acquisition. Think of some indirect ways you could acquire users for your organization's services.

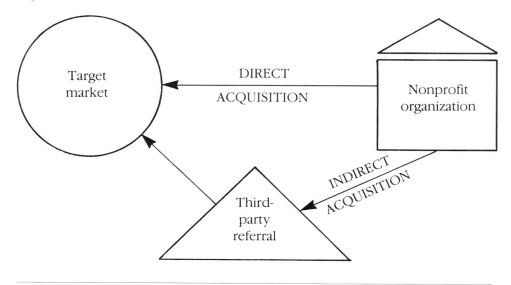

Figure 5: Target Market Acquisition

You can make audience segmentation and target marketing easier by giving each identified target market a name based on its characteristics. For example, you might use humorous names such as Baby Boomers, Upscale Adults, Northeast Rurals, BMW Owners, Gray Power, Blue Blood Estates, Bohemian Mix, Shotguns and Pickups, Tobacco Roads, and so on.

You identify target markets in terms of "who" and "where," that is, all the people who share a particular characteristic or attribute—all 18-year-olds, for example—and who live or work or vacation in a particular area. Thus, a target market for a community college in Pennsylvania might include all 18-year-olds who live in the county. This is geodemography: classification of clusters of actual, addressable, mappable groups of people.

Remember that target marketing is finding the most economical and efficient match between your organization's services and groups of users, current or potential. As is true of many seemingly complex ideas, target marketing has roots in the simple concept illustrated in Figure 6.

It is likely that you will have different groups of target markets if your nonprofit offers many services. Some of these groups may overlap. Some of your services may overlap as well (see Figure 7). For instance, a nonprofit symphony orchestra offers a special series of concerts for young listeners, some of whom are children of adult concert-goers as well. The symphony performs some of the same selections for both audiences. In this overlap, a service (orchestral selection) reaches more than one target market. Communications can be piggybacked. One outreach

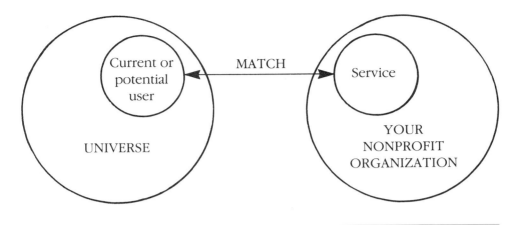

Figure 6: Target Market Relationship to Service

effort may reach both targets (children and adults), and one target market may in-fluence the other in the buying decision. Examine your organization's services to determine which have overlap potential.

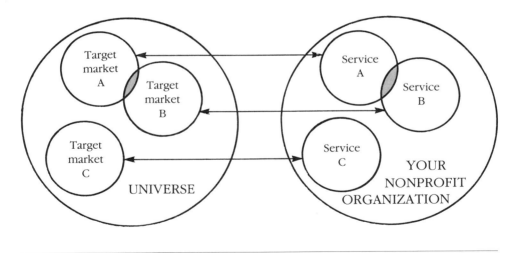

Figure 7: Overlap Potential

You should also consider target market overlap when you are determining mar-keting priorities. To determine marketing priorities, you will need to know the size of each target market group and how much time and money the people in that group have available to devote to your services. Overlap possibilities should be high on your marketing priority list because they will reach more people with equal—or less—expense and effort. Accessibility is important too. You need to de-

29

cide how to communicate with each market segment, that is, what form of media (newsletters, magazines, direct mail, newspapers, radio, TV) you should use.

Marketers also speak of marketing synergy. This is the "boost" that occurs when two or more outreach efforts interact on a target market. One effort rides the wave of the other. The result is greater than the sum of the combined efforts. For an example of marketing synergy, let's look at a promotional campaign designed to achieve marketing goals for a health care organization. The organization uses mass media advertising (television, radio, or newspapers) to communicate awareness of the institution and its services. This effort is coordinated and combined with direct mail efforts for the health care system's new preventive medicine center. The mass media message combined with a direct mail piece describing new preventive medicine services has a supercharged effect on the consumer—this is marketing synergy.

Think of ways that you can apply the concept of marketing synergy to your promotional and advertising efforts.

Networking is another useful strategy in target marketing. Networking is similar to overlapping since it seeks opportunities to piggyback services with other noncompetitive providers. You will save time and money if you can overlap the promotion and delivery of your offering with the promotion and delivery of offerings of other noncompetitive nonprofit or profit-making organizations or even of your own organization. Networking can also provide great marketing opportunities. For example, a director of marketing for a symphony orchestra could use a mailing list of evening concert patrons to promote a summer tour, sponsored by the orchestra, that will visit the opera houses of Vienna. This is overlapping to achieve internal networking.

External networking is when a nonprofit organization such as a civic organization joins forces with a corporation in the community in the delivery of a service that benefits both organizations. For instance, a hospital could offer cardiovascular screenings for the employees of a local corporation. The corporation benefits from its participation in networking by helping employees toward a healthy lifestyle. It helps itself by improving employee attendance and productivity. The hospital promotes its services through this contact with a new segment of its market.

Many nonprofit marketers forget a critical target market: internal constituents. A college, for example, has critical internal audiences: faculty, staff, students, parents, administrators, and board members. Current students and parents may influence prospective students, for example. Likewise, faculty have great influence as they represent their institution to external constituents.

Think about your nonprofit's internal target markets. Use Worksheet 4 to identify your target markets. What do you need to do to enlist their support for your marketing activities? Use Worksheets 5 and 6 to plan your marketing efforts.

Target marketing forces a nonprofit organization to discover that it cannot be all things to all people. When you segment a universe into discrete target markets, you are better able to understand how consumers in the different markets perceive your nonprofit's services.

Worksheet 4

Target Markets

Your organization's services	Target market A	Target market B	Target market C	Target market D	Target market E	Target market F

1. In the left-hand column, list each service your organization offers or is planning to offer. Services should be based on research and not, as is often the case with many nonprofits, on internal guesses on what services should be offered. Consider *consumer* perceptions of your services.

2. List each target market. Explain why the target market is interested in each service. Write down motivational factors.

3. When completed, this worksheet will help you plan your services. It will help you think of target market combinations to market services more effectively and efficiently. It may suggest joint programs or ways to piggyback one program onto another to gain target market share. It will help you cut across the vertical boundaries of your organization.

Worksheet 5

Marketing Time-line Monthly Calendar*

Service	J	F	M	A	M	J	J	A	S	O	N	D

1. List each service. For each service, plot the months it will be offered to the marketplace. Use X for months in which marketing efforts will be aggressive. Use O for months that represent weak marketing efforts.

2. Use this marketing time-line calendar to study service marketing relationships. Look for opportunities to piggyback marketing efforts for services that overlap in time or in target market.

*You may decide to plan a time-line based on your organization's fiscal year, which may not be the same as the calendar year.

Worksheet 6

Using Target Markets to Achieve Marketing Results

1. Look over the two preceding worksheets (Worksheets 4 and 5).

2. Identify target market overlaps.

3. Identify overlaps in your organization's services.

4. Identify opportunities that result from target market overlaps.

5. Identify opportunities that result from overlaps in services.

6. Identify other noncompetitive groups or organizations that may be candidates for services or promotional networking.

7. Identify key internal target markets. How can you enlist them to help achieve marketing objectives?

Chapter 6

Applying Research to Achieve Marketing Results

R esearch is the marketer's best friend. This chapter introduces you to some basic marketing research concepts. It is not a do-all, end-all chapter on market research methodologies. You will need a lot more study before you feel expert in research and its application to your nonprofit's service.

At first, the idea of research may seem overpowering. Research means piles of computer paper containing massive amounts of information that seem almost impossible to digest. Research seems so complex, so number-driven, with little, if any, down-to-earth value. How can research be reduced to the kind of practical information you need to plan and execute marketing for nonprofit services?

And why is research so important to the person marketing a nonprofit? One reason is that you can use research to break the mold of inside-out thinking and action. Research can help a nonprofit organization better understand itself and better understand external (as well as internal) constituents.

In many cases, research is the tool you have to use to justify change. Most people can accept change when they understand the reasons for it. Research can give you those reasons; it can provide you with proof that your changes are rational and carefully thought out, not merely whimsical ideas of your own. Research is also a wonderful tool when you want to justify ongoing activities—if, of course, they deserve to be justified.

Most importantly, research is the way to discover new opportunities. Research can help you explore new concepts, ideas, strategies, approaches, and plans. It can provide you with your own crystal ball.

As a nonprofit marketer, you can take one of two approaches to research: You can say, "Oh, my God, it's too complicated!" and hire an outside firm or consultant to do your research for you. Or you can say, "It's not *that* hard," and undertake to do all or part of it yourself. In any event, this chapter is intended to help you begin to discover that research can be very helpful and to introduce you to the wonderful world of research opportunities.

A word of caution if you elect the "Oh, my God" approach: Many research firms have discovered nonprofit organizations as a great opportunity—for their own profit. As a result, many such organizations will be happy to sell you their services (usually at significant cost). Be cautious. Get estimates and compare costs to make sure you are purchasing services at a fair price. Or you might choose to use the services of a person who formerly worked at a nonprofit of the same type as your own and has started his or her own research firm. Such a person often understands your specific problems and needs and can provide helpful (and cost-effective) services.

Don't misunderstand me. I don't mean to imply that you should stay away from the many excellent commercial research firms out there to help you. Instead, I'm suggesting that you choose the firm wisely. Pick up a trade journal in your nonprofit field to find out who these firms are. Then call colleagues to determine which research organizations are the best ones. Or ask associates at a meeting of your professional organization about their experiences with commercial research firms. Another source of information is your local chapter of the American Marketing Association. Many members represent marketing research firms.

If you have your organizational leaders' approval to take this route and you are lucky enough to find a firm that understands your type of nonprofit and charges rates your organization can afford, you can relax and look forward to a wealth of useful research material. If, however, your organization's leaders are not convinced that research will help them (they are inside-out people), you may have to take the do-it-yourself approach. This chapter is designed to help you do that. But remember, research is a complex subject requiring study and expertise. Use the bibliography at the end of this chapter to sharpen your understanding of research.

Whether you are contracting for research or doing it yourself, this brief overview will be helpful.

Let's begin with a definition: Research is the systematic gathering, recording, and analyzing of data designed to answer questions in an objective and accurate manner. Research can be *quantitative* or *qualitative*.

Quantitative research uses mathematics and statistics to analyze data and quantify relationships between variables; often this is done by using computer analysis.

Qualitative research yields clues but not evidence. Because the findings are not as "hard" as those from quantitative research, qualitative studies (such as focus group research) are often the first step in a more exhaustive research study. Put another way, quantitative research deals with projectable findings; qualitative research deals with measuring and defining issues.

Research can be either *primary* or *secondary*. When you do studies (or have them done) relating to your own organization's specific problems, this is primary research. If you use research that someone else has already gathered for some other purpose, this is secondary research. For example, information from the U.S. Census, which has been done by the federal government, is secondary research data. Using secondary research can save you time and money. Follow the basic rule: Don't attempt to do primary research if secondary research can do the job.

Where do you find secondary research? Start at a library. A careful search of your local public library will yield amazing amounts of helpful, free information. There you will find references (bibliographic indexes) to market research. Ask your librarian to help you. The librarian may suggest a publication called *United States Government Publications: Monthly Catalog*, which lists documents published by all branches of the U.S. government.

Predicasts, a catalog of available market research reports, is also available at your local library or at a college or university library. The bibliography at the end of this chapter will help you identify other useful references.

Use information gathered by federal, state, regional, community, and professional agencies and organizations. Census data will yield demographic information about those who live in geographic locations in your target markets. Trade associations, publications, research foundations, commercial groups, other business and nonprofit firms, as well as (of course) your own professional organization, are excellent sources for secondary information. Create a card file or a computer list of secondary research sources that are, or may be, useful to your nonprofit. This list will be a valuable tool when you are answering marketing questions.

If you search all the appropriate secondary sources and do not find the kind of data you need, you will have to conduct primary research. There are five possible sources for the information you need:

- your organization itself;
- people who are directly or indirectly involved in your services;
- people who have used—or may use—your services;
- your competitors; and
- outside specialists in market research.

Before you decide how to get your information and from whom, you must determine what it is you need to know. You may, for instance, want to find out how a certain group of people (a target market) feels about a specific service, location, or promotional effort. You may want to evaluate a new location before you lease space. You may want information about pricing a service. You may simply want reactions to a new idea, concept, or service.

Whatever your specific information needs, you will find marketing research essential in these four important activities:

- strategic planning;
- assessing attitudes and perceptions before determining future directions;
- looking at trends in your organization, service category, or community; and
- judging the success or failure of specific services.

Timing

When should you do market research? You can see from the list above that some research activities should be done on a regular and ongoing basis. Other research should occur before important decisions are made or after a change in organizational direction (to measure the results).

Frequency

How often should you do research? Experts recommend that health care organizations, for example, conduct patient opinion surveys annually and update general community, employee, and medical staff research at least every two years. This recurring research is called benchmark research. It is used to measure, over periods of time, the effects of an organization's marketing efforts.

The competitiveness of your nonprofit may determine how often you need to do research. In your particular field, you may need to measure opinion more frequently—say every six months or even every month. It is important to note that every nonprofit should do research, regardless of whether it is in a highly competitive posture or not. Otherwise your nonprofit organization is forced into taking a passive, production-oriented perspective.

Research methods

Now for the big question: How is primary research done? There are three basic ways of gathering primary research data: experimentation, observation, and surveys. You can also do qualitative research by using focus groups. These methods are not mutually exclusive. A research project may involve more than one method in order to get the best results.

Experimentation. Using experimentation for primary market research, the researcher systematically manipulates one variable while he or she holds all other variables constant. For example, you might decide to increase your advertising budget while keeping all other aspects of a marketing program constant. Or you could lower the price for a specific service while keeping all other marketing aspects constant. In this way, you can assume that a change in results is due to the variable you have changed. Researchers use experimentation to find the best promotional method, best incentive plan, or best price level.

Observation. The researcher using the observation method gathers primary research data physically or mechanically. This usually involves recording information that can be useful in researching a problem. You can learn a lot by assembling physical evidence. Traffic counts can often provide valuable information about a service or event. Counters, cameras, television, and audio recorders are used to gather the data. Some professional researchers use equipment that measures eye movements to determine how people react to advertising or other visual information.

Surveys. Most nonprofits use the survey method of market research to great advantage. The researcher systematically gathers data from respondents through questionnaires or inquiries. There are several ways to conduct survey research—through personal interviews, telephone, mail, and self-administered survey instruments.

Personal interview. The personal interview relies on a face-to-face meeting between the questioner and the respondent. Personal interviews can be conducted door-to-door or in public places (often called "mall intercepts" since many are carried out in shopping malls). The usual approach is for the interviewer to identify himself or herself to a respondent and attempt to get the respondent to answer a series of questions. The answers may be videotaped, tape-recorded, or written down by the interviewer.

Telephone survey. The telephone survey relies on a person to ask planned questions by telephone. This is a popular survey technique for nonprofits. Its main advantage is speed. Telephone surveys are usually done in relationship to events (a nonprofit marketer might consider doing a telephone survey to measure an advertising or promotional campaign). Telephone surveys can be very selective as well. The research instrument (questionnaire) can be designed to screen the respondents by asking a series of carefully planned questions to get the right target market representation. For instance, the questionnaire might be designed to reach mothers under the age of 35 who live in a certain part of town.

Mail survey. Generally, the mail survey is a questionnaire complete with instructions and a self-addressed envelope for return. It is most often sent to each member of a target group sample selected at random, but it could also be sent to a quota sample (see "Choosing the sample" below).

A mail survey is self-administered (no personal interaction occurs between the respondent and interviewer). The exception is a telephone/mail combination survey used to measure complex issues that require substantial explanation or when it is vital that the survey is absolutely unbiased. The telephone is used to lead the respondent through the mailed questionnaire.

For most mail surveys, however, respondents fill out questionnaires and mail them back at their convenience. Mail surveys take a long time for execution. You should allow at least four weeks. Frequently reminder cards and/or a second letter and questionnaire are sent to encourage the respondent to action.

Since mail surveys are often used by nonprofits, this chapter includes two excellent articles on mail surveys by Cletis Pride, vice president of the National Geographic Society.

Self-administered survey. The self-administered survey can be a printed questionnaire that you do not mail but, instead, administer in a setting. For example, if you work in student recruitment for a college, you might use a self-administered survey during freshman orientation.

Another popular method of doing a self-administered survey is by computer. The respondent keyboards in his or her answers to the questions that appear on the terminal. The advantage is that this method of surveying can be used to deliver a questionnaire to many locations by using portable terminals or multiple software questionnaires.

Choosing the sample. Researchers rarely attempt to gather information from all members of a target group. When all sources are contacted in a survey, the results are called a census. But unless the number of sources is quite small, the costs for such a comprehensive survey are too great to be practical. Instead, you must select a representative group of the universe you are planning to survey. This representative group is called a *sample.* In order to make sure the results are unbiased, it is essential that each member of your universe has an equal chance of being chosen for the sample. When that happens, the result is called a *simple random sample*.

For example, if you want to survey a simple random sample of students at a university, first you must get a list from the registry of all the students. Assign each student a number and then use a table of random numbers to select the members of your sample. There are publications to help you do this. The Rand Corporation publishes a book called *A Million Random Numbers with 100,000 Normal Deviates* (New York: Free Press, 1955). It's not very exciting reading, but it is an excellent way to ensure that your survey will be objective.

A second method of obtaining a random sample is by area sampling. Here blocks, instead of individuals, are selected at random for the survey. Then everyone on the selected blocks is interviewed or, in some cases, respondents are selected from each designated block.

In certain cases, you may want to use a *quota sample* instead of a random sample. A quota sample is most often used when one or more of the components being measured constitute too small a share of the universe to be adequately represented by random sampling. A quota sample is deliberately nonrandom. Using a nonrandom sample increases the probability for selection in order to produce a sufficient sample for reliable projections. The researcher assigns factors to ensure appropriate probability of selection. Surveyors use a quota sample to produce valid and reliable (projectable) data for each segment or component being measured.

The focus group. One of the most popular forms of qualitative market testing now being done by many nonprofits is the focus group. A focus group consists of eight to 12 people who represent the target market being studied. These people are encouraged, either by cash payment or by some other incentive, to come to a meeting, which is usually held at some neutral location rather than the nonprofit organization. A leader takes the group through a series of general questions to get insights into the participants' attitudes, beliefs, and opinions about the subject at hand. The leader may be the marketing director or someone very familiar with the nonprofit organization, but it is better to have a neutral party as the leader so that the group's reactions will be as honest as possible. People hesitate to criticize a product or service to the person offering it.

Focus group market testing is often done to gain broad answers to questions that do not require extremely accurate responses. Group discussions are useful for generating ideas and for developing a quantitative questionnaire.

Focus groups are not good arenas in which to measure specific, detailed items. They are better for measuring broad issues and topics.

Typically, as in market research of all sorts, the focus group leader asks questions that move from the general to the more specific.

The sessions usually last an hour or so. The focus group's responses are videotaped (through a one-way mirror) or audiotaped. Participants are told that their responses are being recorded for research purposes. These recordings are later edited and used as informational or training instruments for the nonprofit organization.

A word of caution: Focus group discussions are useful tools for qualitative research, but they fail to satisfy most of the demands of a quantitative study. Groups, by definition, are not large-scale research studies. Since they are small in number, they have a sampling variation that is large, probably too large to allow the research-er to draw any meaningful conclusions. Be careful not to disguise focus group find-ings as quantitative research and claim a greater validity than exists.

Also, focus groups are not usually the result of random selection. Group par-ticipants are people who are available on the night of a discussion, willing (and able) to get to a discussion facility, and (often) easily reachable, either through a nonprofit's data bank or because they happened to be home to answer the phone. For focus group discussion, therefore, nothing approaching a probability sample is recruited, and response rates are too low to add confidence to the analysis.

Nevertheless, focus groups are popular because they are relatively inexpensive, and they let you tap into the interests and concerns of your target publics. The rich-ness of the responses helps you flesh out the numbers you get from other surveys.

Focus groups are used to plan more extensive quantitative research or to get responses to ideas such as advertising headlines, promotional layouts, or new products. For example, the marketing director of a health care organization wants to know how referral physicians feel about a new Women's Center. A manager of a symphony orchestra would like to find out how audiences feel about a planned series of experimental contemporary music performances. A humanities depart-ment chair at a university wants to determine student reaction to a computer-based educational program. The administrator at a zoo wants to know how people would react to extended hours. Each of these situations is a good candidate for focus group primary research testing.

Selecting a survey method

Which survey method is the best for you? In choosing the best method, you should consider these seven factors:
- accuracy (validity and reliability);
- cost;
- speed;
- amount of data required;
- response rate;
- flexibility; and
- control.

Not all these factors may be relevant to your situation, and there may be others you need to take into account that aren't on the list.

Accuracy. You must determine how accurate your data must be. Mistakes in data may result from a poorly designed questionnaire. Respondents may not un-derstand the questions. The way you organize your questionnaire and the order of the questions are very important. If you've never done surveying before, you may want to ask an expert to help you develop the questionnaire. A good source for help may be your local college or university. Call the business administration department and ask if there is a marketing professor. He or she may be able to help

Survey Methods Characteristics and Criteria

Characteristics/ criteria	Mail survey	Telephone survey	Personal interview	Focus group
Cost	Low	Medium/low	High	Medium
Response rate	Low	High/medium	High	High
Completion time	Medium	Low (shortest)	High (longest)	Low/medium
Versatility	Low	Medium	High	High
Amount of information	Medium	Low	High	Medium
Clarity for respondent	Low	Medium	High	High

you. Often marketing classes take on research surveys as part of their course work.

Remember that key issues of accuracy are validity and reliability. Validity asks the questions: Are your findings *internally* correct? Has the method you've used induced false responses? For instance, have you asked a question that, because of its nature or the respondent's sensitivities, results in false information?

Reliability relates to projectability. Has your survey fairly represented the population you are measuring? Have there been response biases? For example, if you were to do a telephone survey targeted exclusively at low-income groups, you might get false readings because, in many areas, this target group may not have telephones in great enough numbers to ensure representative responses.

Cost. Whatever your situation, cost is probably a major consideration. It is the main reason why many nonprofits tend to use mail and telephone surveys. Survey costs vary depending on the necessary response rate, the length of questionnaire, the quality and quantity of information desired, and the location of the survey subjects. How quickly you need the survey results will also affect the cost; can you piggyback the survey onto another mailing going out next month or did you need it by yesterday? How you reach your survey subject (interviews, phone, mail) affects costs. Rapidly escalating postal costs (outgoing and return) are driving up the cost of a mail survey, but this is still the least expensive approach for a large survey.

Speed. If speed is important, you should consider which survey form can be completed in the shortest time. Telephone surveys are good because they can be done quickly. A room of callers can carry out a telephone survey in a relatively short time. However, cost may be a concern if you need responses outside your local calling area. Telephone interviews are typically executed in about 15 minutes. It is often difficult to keep a respondent on the telephone for longer than that. Mail and personal interview surveys may take a long time depending on how many people will help do the surveying, how many people need to be surveyed, and the location of the people to be surveyed.

Amount of data required. Select the type of survey that will give you the amount of data you'll need. For example, a focus group is unlikely to give you good information about the effect of raising your fees or changing prices for services. A mail questionnaire has the potential for yielding large amounts of information. If, for instance, you needed to conduct a national survey, a mail approach would be a good way to do it. Whereas personal interviews with a national sample may be prohibitive in cost, the mail survey researcher can reach each potential respondent less expensively. Costs may be misleading, however, since the response rate for such a study may be low, depending on respondent interest and the length of the questionnaire.

Response rate. Response rate refers to the number of interviews or questionnaires that are successfully completed. In other words, divide the number of completed interviews or questionnaires by your sample size to get the response rate.

The reliability of your responses depends on your ability to project accurate, representative information from incoming returns as compared to the outgoing sample. (The outgoing sample is the representative group you are measuring.) Professional researchers determine demographic characteristics of the outgoing sample. When returns come in, they measure demographics of the returns against the outgoing sample. If discrepancies exist, they apply weighting factors—factors that are designed to bring the responses back into balance when compared to the outgoing sample.

Professionals are aware of traditional factors that exist in the marketplace and that these factors will affect the response rate. For example, they know that sex and location of the respondent will affect the response rate: Single men living in urban areas will not respond as well as married men living in rural areas; married women living in rural areas will respond better than single women living in urban areas; and women are more likely to return a completed questionnaire than men are.

Much depends on the character of your audience as well as the subject and form of your questionnaire. Interviewer skill is important. It's hard to say which survey method delivers the best response rate. That depends on many issues. The mail survey usually ranks lower in response rate only because some of the other forms can rely on call-backs to get answers.

Flexibility. Flexibility may be important. The personal interview is the most flexible survey method because a skilled interviewer can adjust his or her questions to the respondent's reactions. All senses—sight, hearing, movement (body language)—can be used to carry out the successful personal interview. The focus group method is also flexible; the leader can modify his or her plans to adjust to changing and sometimes unanticipated conditions. He or she can pursue leads that come up in conversations.

Control. How much control do you need? Control refers to the degree to which you can keep tabs on the sample in terms of how well it represents the total universe (all the people in that target market). For example, when you do a telephone survey, you must remember that some telephone numbers are unlisted and that lower-income families are not well represented among telephone owners. Other common problems include dirty (inaccurate) mailing lists and interviewers who may skew the respondents' responses.

Data analysis

Market research, like marketing itself, is a process. It's one thing to gather data through the surveying methodologies covered above, but it is another to analyze these data and draw meaningful conclusions. Therefore, when you begin to plan market research for your nonprofit, you must include ideas for how the information will be analyzed.

Marketing research is often cross-tabulated by computer analysis to gain valuable information. For example, if you have asked respondents to indicate their sex and age, you can use cross-tabulation to find out what young women think compared to young men, older women, older men, and so on. Data analysis is the important "bridge" between surveying, finding, and reporting results.

Format for the research report

When you have compiled and analyzed your research data, you must determine how to prepare it so it will be most useful. It should be reported in both narrative and statistical form. Most market research reports have the following components:

- executive summary (very short copy, key points of the report highlighted);
- narrative report (description of methodology, recommendations, and prioritization of results); and
- statistical support information.

As you devise a format, remember that your objective is to make the information easy to use. It should be both comprehensive and readable. Your organization's executive team will use the marketing research information, and it will form the basis not only for your marketing plan but for your long-range strategic development plan as well.

To sum up, research can be your best friend in helping you market your nonprofit's services. It gives you the information necessary to make careful, thoughtful, knowledgeable decisions that may have tremendous marketing value for your organization. Increasingly, nonprofits need market research. Such research needs to be focused on specific services and economic results. It is more productive the more directed it is in its objectives. This chapter has been designed to whet your appetite for market research, to encourage you to further study, and to lead you to discover the power of research for your nonprofit organization.

For further reading

Check your library for books about marketing research. Many publications can help you plan, prepare, and execute effective market research. Here are a few to consider.

Blankenship, A.B. *Professional Telephone Surveys.* New York: McGraw-Hill, 1977.

Cochran, William G. *Sampling Techniques*, 2nd ed. New York: John Wiley & Sons, 1963.

Council for Advancement and Support of Education. "What Is Market Research? What Can It Do for Me?" CURRENTS, May/June 1982.

Dillman, Don A. *Mail and Telephone Surveys: The Total Design Method.* New York: John Wiley & Sons, 1978.

Erdos, Paul. *Professional Mail Surveys.* New York: McGraw-Hill, 1970.

Ferber, Robert, ed. *Handbook of Marketing Research.* New York: McGraw-Hill, 1974.

Francis, J. Bruce, ed. *Surveying Institutional Constituencies.* San Francisco: Jossey-Bass, 1979.

Goldstein, Sherry, and Kravetz, Ellen, eds. *Findex: The Directory of Market Research Reports, Studies and Surveys*, 5th ed. New York: Find/SVP, 1983.

Kress, George. *Marketing Research*, 2nd ed. Reston, VA: Reston Publishing Co., 1982.

Lindenmann, Walter. *Attitude and Opinion Research: Why You Need It/How to Do It,* 3rd ed. Washington, DC: Council for Advancement and Support of Education, 1983.

McGown, K.L. *Marketing Research: Text and Cases.* Cambridge, MA: Winthrop Publishers, 1979.

Payne, Stanley. *The Art of Asking Questions: Studies in Public Opinion.* Princeton, NJ: Princeton University Press, 1954, 1980.

U.S. Department of Commerce, Bureau of Economic Analysis. *Business Conditions Digest.* Washington, DC: U.S. Government Printing Office, monthly.

Vichas, Robert P. *Complete Handbook of Profitable Marketing Research Techniques.* Englewood Cliffs, NJ: Prentice-Hall, 1982.

The following is an excellent article on do-it-yourself mail surveys. Many of the points in this chapter are covered in this description of mail survey market research and the accompanying guidelines by Cletis Pride, vice president of the National Geographic Society in Washington, D.C.

Let's Take a Survey

"Let's do a survey!" is heard far more often today than it used to be. And with shouts of "chi square!" and "sampling error!" grown men and women sit down to select samples, construct questionnaires, pretest, analyze data, and generally lie to one another in social sciencese.

I know because I do it myself. You can do the same. How could you possibly go wrong in doing a survey? Let me count the ways: wrong questions, badly worded questions, bad sample, nobody answering, etc., etc., etc.

The most dangerous pitfall, though, may be in placing too much confidence in the method. A major weakness of the scientific method lies in the fact that by trying to measure something, we often change it. What you have in your "perfect" survey is what opinions people would have if they were asked for their opinions.

Prior to being asked, Mr. and Ms. Responder may never have given a thought to the question you raised. Or they may have idly mulled it over a bit and decided the answer was "so-so." Now you've asked them to be for it or against it. So they quickly construct strong opinions just for you; then they cuddle them up to their egos and cling to them come hell or high water.

If we were going to be perfectly honest, we'd first try to find the exact boundaries of public apathy on the particular subject that we know to be of life-and-death importance. You can do this by asking questions like: Did you ever hear of the *Doubledome Nonprofit Organization Quarterly Report*? And do you give a damn? Answers to such questions tend to be discouraging. Which is why many researchers omit the "no opinion" column from survey instruments.

Don't overestimate the knowledge of people you are surveying. And don't overestimate your ability to "educate" them. Scandalous as it may seem, you'd find a sizable percentage of the people in your town don't know the name of your nonprofit organization's president. A good many people who have received your publication for years probably know none of the names on the masthead, including the exact name of the publication in question.

Unforgivable ignorance? Maybe so, maybe not. The average person— even the loyal nonprofit supporter—has problems of his or her own. People worry about their income tax, the funny noises in the transmission, what the boss really meant by those remarks, and why their children are always burning incense in their rooms. Things like that keep them from giving your organization the undivided attention it deserves.

Anyway, you may want to consider making provisions in your survey for "don't knows" and "no opinions." It may give you a more accurate idea of the true state of things out there. And it may get you a higher rate of response in the case of mail questionnaires. I'd also recommend using questions that measure the intensity with which opinions are held. Don't go into a survey without asking yourself some questions—and answering them candidly. Such questions as: What problems am I trying to solve? Do I need to take a survey to solve them?

If you decide to do a survey, first state your objectives—in writing. What is it you want to find out? If you can't answer that in a few sentences, turn back. If you don't know what you want, you won't know when you've got it.

If you do know just what you want to find out, the next thing to decide is whom to ask. In your case, it may be all those who take advantage of one of your services or who receive your newsletter. We people in the trade call this the universe.

Now you can send your questionnaire to your entire universe, either by mailing it to everybody or by binding it into a copy of your nonprofit newsletter. I don't recommend either though. It's too expensive if you mail to everyone and too inaccurate as an insert.

So I cast my vote for random sampling. The thing to remember when taking a random sample is that everyone in your universe should have an equal chance of being asked. Otherwise, you may be introducing bias—and that's a four-letter word.

If you use random sampling, a very, very small sample can accurately reflect the opinions of your entire universe. George Gallup and Lou Harris can use a sample of 1,500 voters, for example, to predict a presidential election within a couple of percentage points. The size of the sample does not have to increase proportionately with the size of the universe. If your universe is 200 people, you should sample about 105. If your universe is 5,000, a sample that gives you 210 responses will be adequate. If the universe doubles—to 10,000—your sample should go to around 215. For 100,000, it should be about 220. So for your purposes, you would rarely need more than 250 responses—provided the sample is scientifically pure.

How do you take a random sample? It's not as tough as your friendly neighborhood sociologist says it is. A book of random numbers or even a pair of dice—sometimes both—will help. Did you ever see a book of random numbers? Rand Corporation publishes one [*A Million Random Numbers with 100,000 Normal Deviates*, New York: Free Press, 1955]. It has one million sets of five-digit numbers, covering hundreds of pages—all selected by a computer. I've read most of it. It's duller than a "Gilligan's Island" rerun. It's a handy tool for a big survey, but for most purposes the table of random numbers found in the appendix of most statistics books will do.

Let's assume our universe is 10,000 and we want a sample of 215. If we're doing a mail survey, we should probably draw about 450 names from our list to be sure we get 215 responses. That means we're going to send a questionnaire to every 22nd member of the universe. We could count to 22, pick that name, count to 44, pick that name, and so on. That's not the best way, though, because it's not exactly random. Instead, go to your random number table and find the first number between 1 and 22. That will be the first name in your sample. Then take the 22nd name after that, and so on, until you've got all 450 names. That'll make you eligible for the good statistician's seal of approval. My own sampling for a West Virginia University survey involved a random numbers book, a pair of dice, and a 15-inch ruler.

Now that we have a sample, let's work on a questionnaire. Keep it short and sweet. Ask no extraneous questions. Your survey probably should stay under 20 questions. Your goal should be a questionnaire that can be answered in five minutes. You may want to use a colored stock and even some illustrations. Be sure to enclose a stamped return envelope.

It's best to use structured rather than open-ended questions. If they can check a box or circle a number, they're more likely to answer than if they have to write an essay. It also is going to be much easier for you to analyze. However, you may want to leave room at the bottom for general comments. These can be used to add some human interest when you're writing up results.

Let's not just find out whether our people say "yea" or "nay." Let's find out how intensely they feel about it. In the WVU survey, we had numerous questions asking if people are "very satisfied," "satisfied," "dissatisfied," "very dissatisfied," or have no opinion on specific programs or activities.

By structuring the questionnaire as tightly as possible, we were able to measure attitudes and opinions on 73 subjects—all on a four-page form.

Wording the questions is a tougher job than you might think. You're in trouble if your question means one thing and the respondent's answer means something else. Don't use exotic words, unless absolutely necessary. Don't use words that have two or more meanings. But if you must use them, be sure the context makes the meaning clear. Stay away from loaded questions and dead giveaway words. Don't ask if your nonprofit can do a better job. The answer, of course, is "yes"—but that kind of answer doesn't help you much. Remember that hypothetical questions are likely to produce hypothetical answers. Factual questions produce factual answers. When you're asking multiple choice questions, be sure your respondent knows to check only one answer. Don't ask double-barrelled questions. A "yes" or "no" question like "Would you like to receive the newsletter once a week, or is that too often?" is tough to answer.

Pretests can save your life sometimes. Send your questionnaire to half a dozen people outside your office and ask them to complete it and offer suggestions. They may show you where some of the questions aren't as clear as they might be.

Several years ago a fellow named Stanley Payne wrote a book called *The Art of Asking Questions: Studies in Public Opinion*. If you're going to do a survey, you should read it. It may be in your library. If not, order it from Princeton University Press [3175 Princeton Pike, Lawrenceville, NJ 08648, Attn: Order Dept.; $28 hardcover, $9.95 paperback]. It's not only informative but—believe it or not—it's entertaining.

After you've decided a survey is called for, set specific goals for it, selected your sample, constructed and printed your questionnaire, you can begin to worry about whether anybody is going to answer. Fortunately, you don't have to rely on prayer alone. Specialists have been working on this while you slept. They've tested different ways of increasing the response rate and described their findings in long, dull articles published in *Public Opinion Quarterly* and other such journals.

First thing you want to do, in addition to enclosing a return envelope and designing a questionnaire that just begs for completion, is to explain to the respondent how important it is that he or she participate. An accompanying letter carrying a prestige signature can help here. This letter should assure the recipient that he or she will remain anonymous. Many of your garden variety respondents tend to be modest creatures. In higher education, some faculty members and students even carry modesty to the very edge of paranoia. Never put a code number on a questionnaire that goes to a faculty member. The prof will get that hunted look and begin muttering about academic freedom and McCarthyism.

Believe it or not, specialists have found that hand-stamping—preferably with a nice commemorative stamp—rather than metering an envelope makes for a significantly higher response. In fact, the more expensive the postage, the higher the response rate—right up through air mail-special delivery. In fact, at least one study has shown special delivery as having the lowest cost per response of any form of mail survey. You need to have everything possible going for you, so consider such things as hand-stamping and special delivery. On the other hand, a personalized letter—which would seem logical—does not increase response rate and may even reduce it. Maybe it threatens the respondent's anonymity. Better stick with a form letter. A little gift always seems to help. So maybe you'll want to put a calendar or events schedule in the envelope.

Maximum response dictates that you follow up your first mailing. One way that has proved effective is sending out a reminder postcard three days after the original questionnaire. Then wait about three weeks and send a second questionnaire just in case they've lost the first. If you haven't coded your first questionnaires, you'll have to send a second to everyone.

Let's hope that this is going to bring your response rate over the magic 50 percent mark. Anything less tends to be suspect.

Why not send out twice as many questionnaires and settle for 25 percent? Well, it's because of that old boogie man, error. The major weakness of a mail survey to begin with is the unmeasurable error introduced by nonresponders. There is a suspicion that the people who don't answer may differ in some basic way from those who do. Maybe the difference is racial, or economic, or by sex, or by age group. If you get 75 percent response from all over age 40 and 10 percent response from all under 30, you've got a lousy survey. The higher the overall response rate, the less likely that is to happen. When you get over the 50 percent mark, you begin to gain confidence that those not answering are just apathetic, that any answers they might have given would be about the same as from those who did respond. Anyway, this is what we hear from the sad-faced grey people who write for *Public Opinion Quarterly.* They follow up questionnaires sometimes by interviewing a sample of nonresponders.

A mail survey is not the only kind, of course. It's just the cheapest kind. A personal interview survey is somewhat more accurate and much more expensive. Interviewers must be trained. If your interviewers aren't well trained, people may lie to them—for many people do give the answers they feel are most wanted in these circumstances.

A second advantage of the personal interview is that it gives you an opportunity for immediate follow-up on questions. Some people will refuse to participate, but not nearly so many as will fail to return their mailed questionnaires. The fact that people will not feel so confident of remaining anonymous may cause a little inaccuracy. And interviewers may not record answers correctly.

Never try to do the interviews yourself. Most people will balk at telling you to your face that you're doing a miserable job. If you really are, you're likely to come up with an inaccurate—though comforting—survey when you do your own interviewing.

Telephone interviews fit somewhere between mail surveys and interviews as far as both expense and accuracy are concerned.

What you get out of a survey is data, which is a nice thing to have around the office in case some social scientist drops in. But data in its natural state is unattractive. It has to be processed, manipulated, sometimes fondled, occasionally machined. You can do it by hand or—impersonal as it may seem—by computer. All you need is a cross-sort, which is about the cheapest thing a computer knows how to do. The most complicated correlations you're likely to want are any relationships between opinions on the one hand and age, sex, or some other demographic information on the other.

And there's your dehydrated survey. All you need do is add work and worry. You probably have sociologists and statisticians in your town who can help you with a survey. Use them. But don't let them get the upper hand. Above all, don't let them introduce any of their jargon into your questions.

Reprinted from Techniques, *June 1973.*

Guidelines for a Mail Survey

1. Decide what specific problems you are trying to solve. Decide if a survey is the best road to a solution.

2. State—in writing—the objectives of your survey.

3. Decide which group(s) the survey should cover (your universe).

4. Decide on the size of your sample. (a) Remember that sample size does not increase proportionately to the size of the universe. If your universe is 200 people, you'll need 105 responses. If the universe is 100,000 people, you'll need 220 responses. Even with a much larger universe, you will not need many more responses. (b) Remember that a 50 percent response rate is good in a mail survey, so plan a sample at least twice as big as the size of the response you'll need. But you must get at least the 50 percent return to have confidence in the results.

5. Draw your sample, using a random method.

6. Construct your questionnaire. (a) Be brief. (b) Be specific. (c) Pay particular attention to clarity. (d) Use structured (multiple choice) rather than open-ended questions wherever possible.

7. Pretest your questionnaire. Have friends, colleagues, and some representatives of your universe complete the form and suggest improvements.

8. Mail questionnaire. (a) Remember that researchers have found that the more you spend for postage, the greater the response you will receive. First class (particularly with a commemorative stamp) brings greater results than third; even special delivery pays off. (b) Include a stamped, self-addressed envelope and a letter explaining the importance of participation.

9. Mail reminder postcard three or four days after questionnaire.

10. Second mailing of questionnaire (either to nonreponders or to entire sample) should come two to three weeks after first mailing. Again enclose a stamped, self-addressed envelope and a letter explaining the reason for mailing.

11. Tabulate and analyze returns (computer cross-sort helps here).
12. Most important: Apply what you've learned from your survey.

Reprinted from CASE CURRENTS. *Washington, DC: Council for Advancement and Support of Education, May 1977.*

"I wish we knew how our key target audiences really perceive us as compared to our competitors. If we understood their attitudes, we could more effectively—and possibly more economically—position our organization in the competitive marketplace. We could do a much better job of planning and delivering our mix of services. We could even develop new offerings based on anticipated consumer needs!"

Using Research to Determine Institutional Image

This plea is common among nonprofit administrators. They are frustrated at the difficulty of determining the best ways to use valuable, and often limited, resources to identify opportunities and to solve—or avoid—problems.

At Cleveland State University, John A. Muffo, then director of institutional research (now assistant director of institutional research at Virginia Tech), and Thomas W. Whipple, professor of marketing, effectively used market research to study their university's image. First, a private market research firm gathered data through telephone surveys to measure the attitudes of key target audiences. They surveyed six groups:

- the general population from a six-county area;
- undergraduate students enrolled at Cleveland State;
- students accepted for graduate work;
- parents of undergraduate students;
- college-bound high school seniors; and
- high school teachers and counselors.

Muffo and Whipple then used an 11-point scale to measure target audiences' perceptions of attributes, ranging from academic quality to social life. They asked each respondent to rate a group of other local colleges and universities. They tabulated the results to show how respondents rated each institution on each attribute. From the responses of 1,850 people, Muffo and Whipple developed an expectancy-value model. Predicated on the theory that it is possible to measure the way a product or service is perceived, an expectancy-value model is commonly used in consumer marketing studies. The results enable researchers to predict outcomes and to plan changes in services to improve future outcomes.

The expectancy-value model for Cleveland State revealed important discrepancies between the perceptions of those closest to the university and the perceptions of those least familiar with the institution. Key findings included:

- The university was generally perceived as being geographically and economically convenient.
- The institution offered an adequate education.
- Some members of the target audience were concerned about safety.
- Academic reputation, as perceived by the target audiences, provid-

ed a valuable comparison to competitive institutions.

• Members of target audiences valued the social benefits of living away from home.

Muffo and Whipple's study revealed that Cleveland State University was perceived as having a convenient downtown location and modern facilities, charging relatively low tuition, and offering a variety of courses and programs and an acceptable variety of degrees.

But some of the key target audiences perceived CSU's strengths as weaknesses. For example, the general population, potential students, and high school teachers and counselors perceived the downtown location as unsafe and associated with crime. Many viewed the institution as a commuter college with little dormitory space. Some key audiences saw the urban environment primarily as a parking problem. Target audiences felt academic programs and faculty were of adequate but not outstanding quality, providing a level of education acceptable for an urban state university.

The study painted a picture of a university generally perceived as geographically and economically convenient, offering an adequate education, but failing to provide adequate safety, impressive academic stature, and the social benefits of living away from home. Muffo and Whipple found substantial differences in perceptions of those who knew the institution best and those who knew it least, with the former being more positive.

These findings were very helpful in planning future marketing activities. As marketing research had revealed that the quality of the university's faculty was underrated by target audiences, the university could then plan ways to improve the target markets' perceptions. News releases, publications, media events, campus activities, the speakers bureau, and campus events could highlight faculty members. Concentrated efforts, aimed at identified key target audiences, could inform them of CSU's academic strengths. These objectives could be combined with others, possibly admissions and retention objectives, to offset problems or to avoid them altogether.

Research findings of this sort can be used to give direction to a nonprofit organization's overall marketing effort. Research can be used to monitor, evaluate, and predict consumer behavior in the interest of the organization.

Adapted from "The Use of an Expectancy-Value Model in Studying a University's Image" by John A. Muffo and Thomas W. Whipple, Cleveland State University. The paper was presented at the Annual Forum of the Association for Institutional Research in Denver, Colorado, May 16-19, 1982, and is available on ERIC microfiche system (ED 220059).

Worksheet 7

Determining What Research Needs to be Done

1. Describe the marketing question that needs to be answered.

_____

_____

_____

2. Does secondary research exist to help answer the question?
If yes, what is it?

_____

_____

3. If primary research needs to be done, what form of survey method will
you use? Why?

_____

_____

4. How will you prepare the questionnaire? How will you test it?

_____

_____

5. To whom will it be delivered (universe)? Define your random sample.

_____

6. How will the results be accumulated?

_____

_____

7. How will the results be reported?

_____

_____

8. How will the results be used?

_____

_____

_____

Prepare this sheet for each research project you are planning to execute. Involve others on your marketing team in planning research. You may want to develop a research priority list. What do you need to know first? Why? What can wait?

Worksheet 8

Demographic Segmentation Variables

You can subdivide your market on the basis of variables such as age, sex, family size, income, occupation, residential location, education, family life cycle, religion, nationality, or social class. These variables are ways to distinguish groupings in the marketplace. They often form the basis for research planning. The following list is intended to help you segment target markets for research purposes. Circle the variables that apply to your target markets.

Variable	*Categories*
Age	18-34, 35-49, 50-64, 65 and older
Sex	Male, Female
Income	Under $10,000; $10,000-19,999; $20,000-$29,999; $30,000-$39,999; $40,000-$49,999; $50,000-$59,999; $60,000-$69,999; over $70,000
Family size	1-2, 3-4, 5 or more
Education	Grade school or less; some high school; high school graduate; some college; college graduate; graduate study; doctorate
Occupation	Professional and white collar (including managers, government officials, proprietors, clerical personnel, salespeople), technical and blue collar (including foremen, operators, maintenance people), retired people, farmers, students, housekeepers, unemployed
Social class	Lower-lower, middle-lower, upper-lower, lower-middle, middle-middle, upper-middle, lower-upper, middle-upper, upper-upper
Religion	Catholic, Protestant, Jewish, other, none
Race	Black, White, Oriental
Nationality	American, British, French, German, Eastern European, Scandinavian, Italian, Latin American, Middle Eastern, Japanese, etc.

Location	The 9-digit ZIP code allows precise identification of locations
Psychographics*	Lifestyles, attitudes, interests

Note: The categories presented here are intended as a general guide to segmentation. You may wish to create different categories depending on your nonprofit organization, its mission, and its services.

*Psychographics applies ideas of target audience attitudes and feelings related to geographical location. It is one of marketing's newest research sciences.

Worksheet 9

Choosing Your Type of Market Research

Use this worksheet to determine the type of market research you need to develop and implement.

Focus groups

These are directed group (about 10 to 12 people) discussions that are useful in generating ideas or obtaining qualitative insights. Focus group research is often used to plan more extensive and detailed research.

Written questionnaires

These are often used to collect quantifiable information from a large sample of people. No probing is possible. Simple surveys must be used to ensure adequate returns.

Self-administered questionnaires

A printed survey, or one delivered electronically, is used to gather quantitative information. This differs from a focus group where respondents are led through questions and ideas being studied.

Telephone interviews

An interviewer administers a questionnaire over the telephone. This form of research enables the questioner to probe for better clarification and understanding. Generally the shorter the better to ensure full response. Surveys should take about 10 minutes.

Personal interviews

A one-on-one interview that enables in-depth discussion of topics. Used to collect specific information from target audiences.

Informal contacts

Research gained from individual or group discussions with individuals who have market insights or information that will help you answer questions.

Sales personnel

Research gained from structured market information forms or formal/informal weekly meetings to gain the insights of sales personnel on their customers (target markets).

Chapter 7

Analyzing the Competition

For some nonprofit organizations, the mere mention of the word "competition" elicits pained and nervous responses. There's something about the idea of competition that strikes fear in the hearts of many nonprofiters. This is not something new.

For many decades, nonprofits have taken a reactive approach to their work. Traditionally many nonprofit organizations edged forward into new offerings only when "forced" to by competitors. And, for the most part, these competitors were other nonprofits working in the same subject area. Only recently have nonprofits begun to worry about competition from the corporate, profit-motivated sector. In today's world, the idea of competition is a critical, driving force that needs careful study and analysis.

Competition can help you in your attempt to apply marketing concepts to advance your nonprofit organization. You can use competition and competitive forces to understand your organization's strengths and weaknesses. Competitive studies can yield other benefits:

• You can plan future marketing strategies and actions.
• You can improve current services.
• You can drop services that are no longer successful, viable, or relevant.
• You can add new services.
• You can plan promotional strategies.
• You can discover marketing niches—gaps or needs in the marketplace that your services can fill.
• You can plan market research.

Today, a nonprofit marketer should not view competition as a battle between organizations in the same subject area, or even between substitutable services. A much broader, and more appropriate, viewpoint is necessary: *All* competing organizations (whether profit, nonprofit, or government-supported) strive for the attention, support, and dedication of the target market's limited time and money.

Marketing is your organization's "best foot forward"—its attempt to offer its own services to those who will most benefit from them. This broader idea of competition not only forces nonprofits to reassess long-established attitudes but also opens new doors of opportunity.

Developing a competitive strategy

Your organization's services exist in an environment of forces. Some of these forces are created by the user (your target market), some by competitors, and some by your organization itself. To assess these forces, start with an audit of the competition. Find out what is being offered, where, and for what price. The best way to do this is to visit the competition. Experience what is being offered, where it's being offered, and how your competition does business. Take a course, hear a concert, attend a performance. You may find that one of the best ways to get an "outside-in" perspective of your organization is from the vantage point of your competitor. Start a collection of your competitor's promotional materials, newspaper articles, announcements, advertisements, catalogs, and newsletters. Build a library of materials organized by competitor and by services.

Carefully analyze these communications. Your analysis will help you develop a competitive audit. Determine the who, what, where, when, why, and how of each competitive communication:

• *Who:* Describe the target markets your competition is aiming for. Analyze this audience. How does it relate to yours? Are you after the same group? What limits does that place on your potential success? What opportunities does it offer?

• *What:* Analyze your competitor's services. Compare them to yours. Use market research to measure consumer comparative analysis. Do this by measuring consumer perceptions of the strengths and weaknesses of competitive services. Use research to compare competitive services to yours. Do you have a competitive advantage? If yes, how can it be used? If no, what must you do to get one?

• *Where:* Identify your competitor's locations of services. Are these locations convenient for the target audiences? Is location an advantage or a disadvantage when compared to the location of your services?

• *When:* Timing can make the difference between success and failure. From the target audience's viewpoint, compare your competitor's timing of services to yours. Again, use market research to measure timing comparisons. Use the marketing timeline monthly calendar (Worksheet 5, page 32) to compare your timing with that of your competitor.

• *Why:* What target market wants and needs are satisfied by your competition? How do those relate to your services? Is there any overlap, any direct head-to-head competition?

• *How:* What process does your competitor use to plan, create, deliver, and evaluate its services? Compare this to the process your organization uses. Use market research to assess results.

As you would expect, competitive analysis focuses on activities outside your own organization. It is an excellent tool to use to help plan and execute your marketing efforts. It is also less threatening to your staff than an analysis of the strengths or shortcomings of your own organization and its services. It's much more comfortable to analyze others than to analyze yourself. This is the "outside-in" approach compared to the traditional "inside-out" approach of most nonprofits. Nonprofits must find every way possible to adopt "outside-in" marketing perspectives. Competitive analysis is one way to do this.

Competitive analysis serves two important purposes: It helps you improve your "wares" by providing a measure for comparison. And it provides direction (opportunities) by allowing you to identify unfilled needs and wants of the target audience. Competitive analysis has resulted in many new services in the profit-motivated sector as well as the nonprofit world. These two objectives are very important from a strategic marketing perspective. If you achieve these objectives, you will have done much to advance your organization.

Positioning

Each of your competitors probably has a marketing plan and related strategies. Some parts of the competitor's plan may be very similar to yours, and others may be very different. In some places the plans may even overlap. In other places gaps may occur—a specific need is unmet, a particular market is overlooked. When your organization steps in to fill the need or serve the market, what your organization is doing is called "positioning." Position is the niche or place your services occupy, as perceived by target audiences, compared to competitive services. Note that it is not how *you* perceive the position of your organization's services, but how your target audience perceives it. The target audience is the ultimate judge.

Positioning starts with a product—a service. But positioning is not what you do to a service. Positioning is what you do to the mind of the target market prospect. That is, you position the service in the mind of the prospect. And the prospect relates your service to other similar services he or she knows about. That's competitive positioning.

In Figure 8 on the next page, Service A receives "top of the mind" position as compared to Services B and C. Services D, E, F, and G are ranked lower in perception. Note that the illustration is meant to represent a total target audience—the compilation of attitudes and perceptions of many people. In marketing, this represents a "share of mind" concept. In this figure, Service A has the best share of mind. If Service A is your organization's, you've done a good job of marketing your product.

Use Worksheet 10 at the end of this chapter to analyze your competition.

For further reading

Although the two books listed below were written for corporate, hard-product organizations, they provide many excellent ideas about using positioning to win

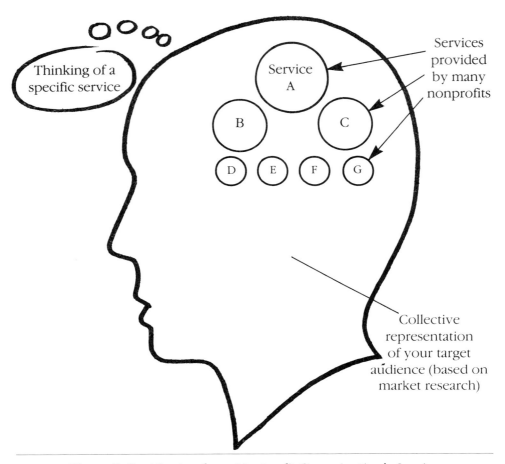

Figure 8: Positioning for a Nonprofit Organization's Services

the battle for recognition in an overcrowded, media-blitzed marketplace. Careful study will help you discover how to apply positioning concepts to your nonprofit organization's services.

Ries, Al, and Trout, Jack. *Marketing Warfare.* New York: McGraw-Hill, 1986.

Ries, Al, and Trout, Jack. *Positioning: The Battle for Your Mind.* New York: McGraw-Hill, 1981.

Worksheet 10

Analyzing Your Competition

1. Perform a competitive audit of services. Remember who, what, where, when, why, and how.

2. Use the 4 P's—product (service), place (location of the service), price, and promotion—to compare your competitor's services to yours. (See Chapter 1, page 2, for an explanation of the four P's.)

3. Use research to determine, from a target audience's vantage point, what position these services occupy.

4. What limitations are forced on your organization as a result of your market position?

5. What opportunities exist? How can you use current market positioning to plan, develop, and deliver new services?

Chapter 8

Trails to Success: Needs Analysis

Marketing success will depend, to a great degree, on how well you understand how your nonprofit's services are perceived by others. You must use marketing techniques (audience segmentation, research, and service evaluation) to examine your organization from the outside in. You need to understand how and why target audiences respond to your organization and its services. Before expending time, effort, and other valuable resources on developing and implementing new services, you must be able to anticipate how target markets will react.

Marketing, in its simplest form, is an exchange process. Someone gives up something in return for something else. Motives for the exchange depend on individual wants and needs.

Think about these questions: What internal *and* external groups have needs to be met? How do these needs relate to your organization's services? How can your organization modify or change its services to better serve the needs and wants of key target groups?

Marketing research plays an important role in assessing the needs of key constituents and determining whether to add, improve, or drop services. Remember that key constituents may include internal as well as external audiences. For example, suppose that you are the chair of the humanities department in a college. You are considering hiring a new art history professor. At present your department does not offer art history courses. Your research of other colleges and universities in your area shows that none has a strong art history curriculum. Further research indicates that high school art teachers would be interested in taking art history offerings for accreditation during the summer.

Thus, you have identified a particular need (for a summer session art history course) of a particular target market (high school art teachers) related to your nonprofit's mission (education). In this example, your need for humanities students could be met by the creation of the new summer session art history course. The needs of "customers" (art teachers) can be met through this new service. The needs of the new art history professor can be met with an opportunity to teach a new course in his or her field of interest.

In this example, you have identified several needs—of your institution, of the new professor, and of the target market. You have created a new service to satisfy those needs. You have arranged a marketing exchange based on needs. In this simple example, you have identified several exchanges: The university exchanges the professor's knowledge for student tuition. The professor exchanges his or her skills and teaching abilities for income and the opportunity to expand interest in the field of art history. The student exchanges tuition payments for teaching credentials and opportunities for advancement. This is a simple example of a marketing needs analysis.

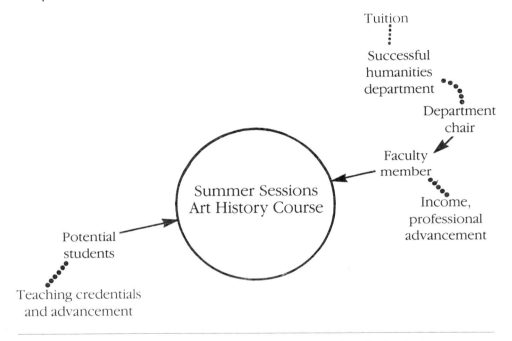

Figure 9: Marketing Exchanges Based on Needs Analysis

A careful needs analysis is essential to networking. You cannot market services to overlapping target markets until you have identified the needs of those markets. Most nonprofits do a poor job of networking. Because nonprofits were traditionally funded, organized, and administered along vertical lines (by units, departments, or sections), there was no need to consider networking for internal or external purposes. Delivery methods were traditional, based on slowly evolving historical precedents. People prepared an assumed service for an assumed audience and delivered it to satisfy assumed needs. But in today's climate, that sort of "assumed" posture can no longer guarantee success. To achieve success, you must use new marketing practices based on careful research.

Consider how you could use needs analysis to network many services collectively. How can one part of your nonprofit organization offer services cooperatively with another part of your organization? What common target audience needs exist to allow this to happen? Use Worksheet 11 to do a needs assessment inventory for your organization.

What kind of needs should you be concerned about? How will you know what needs to research? You will find the best answers to these questions in your nonprofit's mission statement. Review the mission statement you prepared in Chapter 4 (Worksheet 3, page 25) and begin to plan for a careful match between your organization's mission and services and the needs of its internal and external target audiences.

Needs analysis is a powerful tool in your marketing tool kit. It goes to the core of marketing and marketing exchange concepts. As you begin to execute services based on needs, you will be able to plan and apply knowledgeable marketing strategies. You will find evidence that will encourage others, who are used to running nonprofit activities on the basis of "seat-of-the-pants" decision-making, to take a more knowledgeable (and potentially successful) look at the organization, its target audiences, and its services.

Worksheet 11

Establishing a Needs Assessment Inventory

Target market	Needs	Your service

1. List your target markets.

2. Describe needs for each target market.

3. List the service (current or potential) that could be used to satisfy each target market's needs.

4. Share this worksheet with others and add their ideas to your needs assessment inventory.

5. Use this worksheet to plan and execute marketing services. Use research (Chapter 6) to provide information that you can use to help assess, plan, deliver, and evaluate efforts.

Chapter 9

Onions, Umbrellas, and Mosaics: Marketing Techniques to Advance Your Organization's Services

Marketing a nonprofit organization's services is much more difficult than marketing a "hard" product such as an automobile, camera, or appliance. A hard product can be seen, photographed, described, tasted (at least some can), and felt. A hard product is tangible. A nonprofit organization's services are intangible. You can't see, touch, taste, or feel them. They are not easily defined.

The difficulty of marketing the intangible explains why nonprofits have been so slow in accepting marketing, and why, even when marketing is accepted, its application to nonprofit organizations has been difficult and often misunderstood.

The key to marketing your organization is its services—what it has to "sell" or offer for exchange.

The best way to market a nonprofit organization and its services is to combine two approaches—marketing the total organization and marketing a particular service or group of services. In this way, you use three levels of marketing:
- institutional—marketing the generic (collective, whole) organization;
- product line—marketing groups of related services; and
- product level—marketing specific, individual services.

Figure 10 on the next page illustrates these three levels. Note that individual services are categorized and, when viewed together, form a product line. Collectively, product lines relate to form the overall institution.

This concept is important to understand, especially as you plan to promote your organization. The great debate continues: Should a nonprofit promote its collective image (institutional, generic organization), product lines, or individual serv-

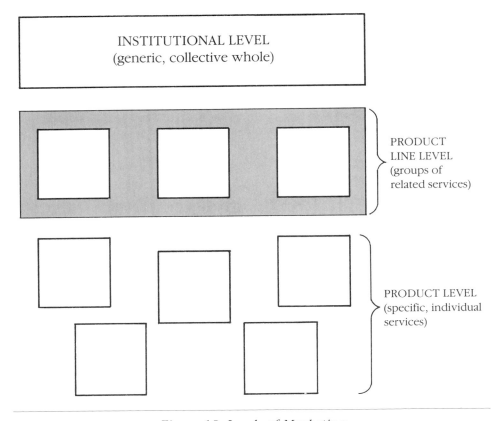

INSTITUTIONAL LEVEL
(generic, collective whole)

PRODUCT
LINE LEVEL
(groups of
related services)

PRODUCT LEVEL
(specific, individual
services)

Figure 10: Levels of Marketing

ices? The answer is, of course, all three.

As the illustration shows, the key to marketing is the services your organization offers. Everything your organization does (and is perceived as doing) can be traced to the individual service or groups of services.

Let's look at these approaches to marketing from another angle. To market the organization, you must attempt to translate the mission into collective, generic, institution-wide marketing. We call this kind of marketing the "umbrella."

Under this umbrella, you market the organization's services so that they relate to, and support, the collective organizational mission. This is marketing at the product level. Next, you find ways to market each group of services as if it were a product line; market these services as a collection of related services with similar characteristics and attributes.

The key to marketing: The service onion

It's essential that you know as much as you can about your organization's services. Since they are intangible, this may not be easy. It may require careful study and research.

Start by using Worksheet 12 at the end of this chapter to identify your organization's services. Focus on each individual service. Use market research, as explained in Chapter 6, to do this. You must know your services as perceived "outside in" (by their users) as well as "inside out." Examine the characteristics of each service as perceived by the key target audiences, both internal and external.

Think of each service as an onion. An onion has many layers, but the core (the part where growth and change originate) is the service itself. Here are some examples of services: for a university, a course; for a symphony orchestra, a symphonic piece; for a health care organization, a medical service; for a fine arts organization, an exhibit; for a city government, a planned tax reform; and for the board of directors of a condominium, the installation of a new security system.

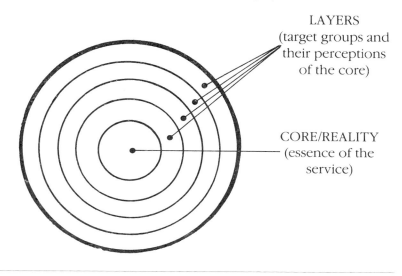

LAYERS
(target groups and
their perceptions
of the core)

CORE/REALITY
(essence of the
service)

Figure 11: Service Onion

Each layer of the onion represents a perception or image of your services held by a target audience. The innermost layer, then, might be the perception of the service held by those who actually create it (internal staff). This layer, closest to the core (or reality), is likely to be the most accurate. The next layer might be the perception of other people in your organization who know about the service but are not directly involved with it. A layer might consist of the organization's administrators, board members, or leaders. Further from the core would be layers representing the perceptions of each target audience and those of third-party observers such as the media, the general public, legislators, benefactors, community leaders, and competitors.

These different perceptions can determine the success or failure of your service. And how well you understand the perceptions or images held by others will determine to a great extent your ability to market that particular service. Your understanding of the service onion will help you make critical decisions on how to "package" (promote and advertise) each service.

The outermost layers of your service onion are apt to be those perceptions that are least accurate. This is important. You will constantly be amazed by how others perceive your services. Sometimes the perception of the service will be better than the service itself. This can be a double-edged sword. It's nice that people believe that your service is better than it really is. But this may lead to backlash when they find out that they were mistaken. The successful marketer recognizes the difference between service reality and target audience expectations and constantly strives to bring reality and expectation as close as possible.

You can also look at this complex idea of marketing by service as a mosaic. Your nonprofit organization is the whole picture. The parts of the picture are product lines (groups of services), and each individual piece is a service. It's your job to understand and market each piece and every section, and to relate them all to the "big picture," the whole organization.

In almost every way, how your organization's services are managed will determine what your marketing covers, how big it is, and how successful it will be. The organization of services, the product lines, and how they relate to form the whole organization constitute the key to marketing (as illustrated in Figure 10). Every aspect of your organization's activities can be traced back to the reality of your individual services. These components are the elements of your nonprofit organization, and they are the simplest components. Management and marketing of the total organization can result from control of the simplest components. Services are critical to the ultimate success of your nonprofit organization.

This concept of service reality and relationship to the whole nonprofit organization, combined with the target audiences' perceptions, forms the basis for marketing a nonprofit organization. This balance of forces, internal and external, can make the difference between success and failure.

Marketing by product lines

Next you must understand your services by categories, by product lines. Identify the ways the services relate—or do not relate—to each other. Plan how they can be categorized, organized, and marketed collectively. You must also understand how your services relate to competitive services as described in Chapter 7.

Institutional marketing

Finally, you must relate your product lines to the total organization. You need to develop ways to use product line marketing to market the whole organization and to position your organization among its competitors. Through positioning, your organization will attempt to seek a competitive advantage, find market niches, and capture market share.

Use information about your organization's services as described in this chapter to build research plans for future development. This knowledge becomes a valuable marketing and administrative tool. Use umbrellas, onions, and mosaics to market your nonprofit organization and its services.

Worksheet 12

Identifying Your Nonprofit's Services

1. Write a description of your institution. Describe the overall purpose of your organization. Use the mission statement you developed in Chapter 4 (Worksheet 3, p. 25). Limit yourself to 50 words or less.

_____ _____

_____ _____

_____

_____

_____

2. List all your individual services.

_____

_____

_____

_____

_____

_____

_____

3. Group your services into product lines. Give each product line a name.

Product Line   **Individual Service**

_____   _____

                                _____

                                _____

(continued next page)

Product Line   **Individual Service**

_____   _____

_____

_____

_____

_____   _____

_____

_____

_____

_____   _____

_____

_____

_____

4. Circulate this worksheet to others in your organization. Ask them for their reactions and, if appropriate, incorporate their responses in your list.

5. Use research to get outside perceptions of your nonprofit organization, its product lines, and services. Prepare a separate sheet listing services and external perceptions of key target market groups.

6. Report competitive services. Use Worksheet 10 in Chapter 7.

7. Use this completed worksheet to form the foundation for a comprehensive marketing plan for your nonprofit organization.

Section 3

The Building Blocks
of Marketing

Chapter 10

Creating and Executing A Marketing Mix

Now that you have learned how to use research and analysis to lay the groundwork for your marketing effort, it's time to develop your own marketing mix—the blend of those principles and practices that will achieve results for your organization. Remember, however, you can't do it alone.

Effective marketing requires the coordination of many efforts. Unfortunately, many nonprofit organizations are particularly poor at cooperative efforts. We have already discussed some of the reasons for this, such as the vertical organization of most nonprofits and the resulting political environment. Issues of "turf" often complicate the situation: Some individuals or departments claim marketing; others reject it. Debate rages on the question, "*Who* will do marketing?" The answer, as always, is "everybody." No one person or department can "do" marketing. Effective marketing is a process that should be pervasive throughout the organization.

Resist pressures to get caught up in the controversy about where marketing should be placed in your organization. Effective marketing requires a formal organizational structure that includes many people with marketing responsibilities. And more importantly, to be successful, marketing requires many skills and the help of many people. For example, public relations or public affairs staffs can contribute significantly, as can business or finance staffs or the comptroller. Promotion and advertising skills are also important. Leadership plays a vital role. Some nonprofits even employ salespeople—although they carry a different title—to achieve results. Effective marketing requires coordinating the efforts of many skilled people, working together to advance the organization.

The marketing process

There are six basic actions in the marketing process:
  1. *Identifying your target markets.* Use market research to develop discrete target

markets through audience segmentation.

2. *Knowing your services.* Use market research to learn how your target audiences perceive your services.

3. *Establishing your market position.* Use advertising, promotion, and public relations to carve a niche in the marketplace for your services. Use market research to measure your market position (as perceived by your target markets).

4. *Nurturing your success.* Make marketing work effectively by identifying and pursuing every opportunity. Cut your losses by finding ways to focus on "stars" while avoiding "dogs." Stars are services offered by your organization that are popular and successful. Dogs are not.

5. *Measuring results.* Use evaluative market research to measure your services as perceived, accepted, or rejected by your target markets. Build on successes.

6. *Planning for the future.* Marketing can assist in program planning and development. It can help you find new opportunities. Constantly measure your organization's mission statement (Chapter 4) against new opportunities.

Developing a marketing plan

By now you are beginning to understand why marketing can best be described as a mix. Many ingredients go into the recipe. These ingredients are not always the same because they are determined by the desired results. For example, you may require extensive market research to plan, execute, and deliver a new service, but a service you've been providing for years may require only minor research to measure its effectiveness and to tune it up. In developing your marketing recipe, first determine the results you need and then consider the marketing options (ingredients) that are available to you. Select those marketing options that will achieve the desired results. Ask yourself some key questions:

• How can I assemble all the ingredients necessary to get the marketing job done?

• What skills and abilities exist within my organization? What assets are available to help achieve marketing results? How can weak areas be strengthened?

• How should marketing be achieved for my organization? Should it be a team approach involving many people? Should teams be organized along product lines? Should a committee be organized to track team efforts?

• What key skills are necessary? Do people in the organization have those skills or will I need outside help? Consultants? Agencies? Research firms?

Your marketing plan should include when and how each step of the marketing process will take place and who will do it. It should include or provide for a skills audit to identify the people—in-house and outside—necessary to the marketing effort. It should have a budget and an action plan calendar.

Your marketing plan should provide the framework for marketing your nonprofit organization and its services. Use Worksheet 13 at the end of this chapter to develop a marketing plan. It should include marketing activities for your organization and its services (Worksheet 14).

Success depends on how good your marketing plan is, so give yourself plenty of time to work on it. Develop the plan carefully. It's important to involve many people in the development of the plan; you will benefit not only from their input but, later, from their support when the plan is put into motion. Unless your plan receives strong universal approval within your organization, it will fail.

Use the planning process to identify and resolve problems. Any marketing-related problems (including basic issues such as what services are to be offered) must be resolved before the plan is put into action. Otherwise valuable resources may be expended that will dilute results. You simply cannot afford a weak marketing plan.

Before you introduce your plan, you need to analyze the political environment in your organization. Use skills learned in Chapter 3 to do this. What roadblocks can you anticipate? How can you get around those obstacles? What opportunities are apparent? How can you network with others to get results? Refer to Worksheet 1 in Chapter 3 (page 19) for those people whose support will be most important to the marketing effort.

Remember that marketing is built on common-sense, practical, results-oriented methods. You can design your marketing effort to be as straightforward or as complex as you want, but it's probably best to start out simply. Even in its simplest form, marketing is a powerful tool. No matter how simple your marketing approach, however, don't take any shortcuts. You will still need to take the six basic steps in the marketing process and to follow the procedures given in Worksheet 13.

Worksheet 13

A Marketing Plan Outline

1. Determine what services are to be marketed. Consider new services as well as existing ones.

2. Use research to evaluate services.

3. Determine how your services are going to reach the marketplace.

4. Segment your universe into target market groups by using market research to determine behavior, needs, wants, and perceptions of your organization and its services.

5. Use market research to determine which features of your services you want to highlight.

6. Find out what barriers exist to marketing each service.

7. Examine each service in terms of what it is, where it is to be offered, and how it will be promoted.

8. Develop a budget for marketing each service. What will it cost to reach each target market?

9. Establish priorities and a time-line schedule for marketing.

10. Evaluate success or failure and start over!

Worksheet 14

Planning Marketing Action

1. List your target markets. Use the skills you have learned to organize the target markets into market segments. (See Worksheet 8, p. 58.)

2. What research needs to be done to analyze existing target markets? To develop new ones? (Use Worksheets 7 and 9, pp. 56 and 60.)

3. What research needs to be done to measure your services as perceived by external target markets? (Use Worksheets 7 and 9.)

4. How can you use your services to establish a position in the competitive marketplace? What product mixes can you offer to target market segments? How can these mixes be used to capture and hold competitive positions as perceived by your target market and segments? (Use Worksheet 10, p. 65.)

5. What do you need to do to ensure continued success for established services? (Use Worksheet 11, p. 70.)

6. What actions are necessary to discontinue services that no longer contribute toward the mission of the organization and the satisfaction of target market needs? (Use Worksheet 12, p. 75.)

7. What marketing research needs to be done? For overall organizational image? For specific services? (See Chapter 6.)

8. What marketing research can you do to find new organizational opportunities? How can you use constituent research to find new target markets? (See Chapter 6.)

Chapter 11

Developing a Promotional Plan

I t is not by accident that this chapter on promotion comes near the end of *Your Personal Guide to Marketing a Nonprofit Organization.* I put it here to emphasize the point that you cannot plan promotion and apply promotional concepts until you have done appropriate marketing research and prepared a marketing plan. Many people who work for nonprofits think promotion comes first or—worse—confuse marketing with promotion. Promotion must grow out of marketing. You cannot prepare an effective promotional plan until you have thoroughly and thoughtfully prepared a marketing plan. The worksheets you prepared at the end of Chapter 10 should form the basis for promotional planning, and you can use Worksheet 15 in this chapter to plan and execute promotional activities.

Many books have been written about the mechanics of advertising and promotion, but few have addressed the promotion and marketing needs of nonprofit organizations. You will not find many models to follow. In many ways, this guidebook breaks new ground. By working carefully, you will be able to guide your nonprofit through the promotional process to achieve success.

The key to success is the wedding of marketing and promotion ideas. Promotion is one of many advancement efforts held together by the "glue" of marketing. These efforts also include public relations, public affairs, development, and advertising, all of which work to achieve strong support for your nonprofit organization and its services.

How does promotion differ from marketing?

Promotion includes the actions your organization employs to reach target audiences. Promotion requires much of the information marketing provides. It cannot be done effectively on its own or for its own sake. If that happens, valuable resources of time and money can be lost. Promotion is the "bridge" that links your organization and its services with its external target markets.

Promotion is the engine that provides power to the marketing vehicle, but promotion requires marketing information to be successful. Marketing information enables you to identify what to promote, to whom to promote it, why to promote it, how to promote it, and when to promote it.

Like marketing, promotion is both a science and an art. Promotion uses qualitative and quantitative market research to achieve best results, but it also requires creativity (often in the form of writing, artwork, and design). Promotion is the integration of creative ideas with applied market research and marketing concepts. The ultimate aim of promotion is to influence target audiences to take positive action toward your organization's services.

Drafting a promotional plan

The best promotional plans are direct results of excellent marketing plans. Attempting to promote services without considering marketing first is sheer folly. Don't be tempted to do it, and—if you can—prevent others in your organization from doing it. The promotional plan should come last in a series of plans developed for your organization:

1. *program plan* (what services will the organization offer?);
2. *business plan* (what is the budget?);
3. *marketing plan*; and
4. *promotional plan.*

You will see why the marketing plan comes before the promotional plan if you look at the steps below that are necessary to develop a promotional plan. Note that you had to go through these steps to prepare the marketing plan.

To promote your services you must:

• understand your organization's mission (Chapter 4);

• use market research to analyze your target markets and your services as they relate to those target markets (Chapter 6);

• understand your organization's services (Chapter 9);

• understand how to do audience segmentation and target market identification (Chapter 5);

• understand why each target market needs and wants your organization's services (Chapter 8); and

• understand competing services in order to position your services in the users' minds (Chapter 7).

A critical element in your promotion is the message—selecting what you should say about your services. A word of warning: Many nonprofits fail miserably at this task because their messages are developed from the inside out, rather than from the outside in. Their messages speak to the people within the organization, rather than to target audiences outside of it. This is where marketing and marketing research play a critical role. Marketing, when properly done, forces you to create promotional messages that speak to the needs and wants of your target markets. Such marketing-inspired promotion greatly enhances results.

Using marketing techniques to promote your services

This guidebook has given you several techniques that you can use in promotion. First, market research enables you to analyze how target audiences perceive your organization and its services. Market research also reveals how your target markets see your organization in relation to its competitors. Now that you have all this information down on paper, it's time to put on your "marketing shoes" and take a walk into your target markets' world. Use your market research to think your way into the mind of a member of your target audience. From this viewpoint, take a long critical look at your organization and its services.

Consider your organization's positioning—how it measures up to competing organizations. Now, still wearing your marketing shoes, put on your creative hat and ask yourself what special aspects, unique characteristics, or unusual features set your nonprofit's services apart from competing services. Look for promotional strategies in these distinctive qualities. Then consider the best promotional vehicles to convey those special qualities to your target market. Your marketing shoes should help you do this.

Promotional vehicles include newspapers, magazines, direct mail, television, radio, billboards (outdoor advertising), posters, and signs. Chapter 12 will help you choose the right promotional vehicles for your services. Chapter 13 covers one of these vehicles—print advertising—in detail.

Once you have selected the methods you will use, you need to decide how to measure the results of these efforts. You can include an action or response method; for example, a newspaper ad might contain a coupon to send in, a radio ad might give a phone number to call, a billboard might promote a box number to contact.

When your promotional efforts are in place, you will need to use market research techniques to evaluate them. You can use the results of the evaluation to improve future promotions or even to improve your organization's services.

Promotion is communication. Marketing promotion is communication designed and executed from a target market's point of view, not from the nonprofit organization's viewpoint!

Integrated marketing promotion

Some nonprofits have chosen to promote an umbrella image for the entire organization in conjunction with the promotion of specific services (Figure 12 on the next page). We call this "integrated marketing promotion."

This technique can be effective because it promotes the overall concept of the organization (its institutional image) and its specific services. You cannot afford to promote one without the other. Both are important. The institutional image presents the overall organization to the marketplace. Under that umbrella, promotional support is provided for specific services.

Marketers know that synergy results when ideas and efforts are planned in tan-

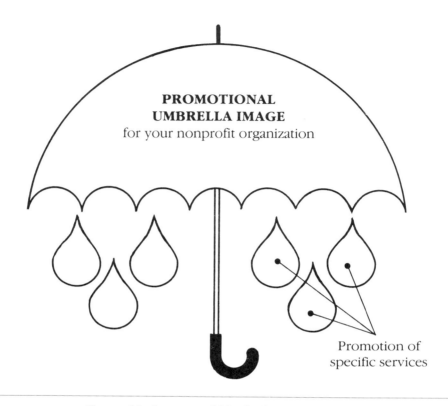

**PROMOTIONAL
UMBRELLA IMAGE**
for your nonprofit organization

Promotion of
specific services

Figure 12: Integrated Marketing Promotion

dem rather than in isolation. Careful integration of services and promotional concepts, based on target market planning and overlap (Chapter 5), will enhance your promotion and increase possibilities of success. Promotional strength is achieved through the careful use of related ideas and concepts.

You are using integrated marketing promotion when you use organizational identity (a symbol or logo for your nonprofit) and/or an organizational slogan in conjunction with the promotion of a specific service. The organizational identifier (symbol or slogan) adds promotional dimension to your efforts. You can tie promotional ideas together with common threads such as a slogan. For example, my organization, Sharp HealthCare, uses the slogan "The Future of Health Care Is Sharp." Every time a consumer uses any product line (group of services), the identifier—logo or slogan—ties the service to the overall organization and reinforces recognition for both service and organization. One service advances another and all promote the umbrella organization.

Timing is critical in promotion, especially when a new or modified service is being introduced into the marketplace. In Chapter 5 you learned how to plot your organization's services on a marketing time-line calendar. This helps you pinpoint overlaps that may create windows of opportunity to piggyback promotional efforts onto other efforts. Don't miss these opportunities for synergy.

There are many ways to promote nonprofit organizations, but none will work if you do not apply marketing concepts. Therefore, your promotional plan should be carefully related to your marketing plan. Consider timing, and use market research to plan, execute, and evaluate your efforts.

For further reading

Book, Albert C. and Schick, C. Dennis. *Fundamentals of Copy & Layout.* Lincolnwood, IL: National Textbook Company Business Books, 1986. "Everything You Need to Know to Prepare Better Ads" is the subtitle for this book. It's an excellent "how-to-do-it" book about writing and designing effective advertising for all forms of media. It includes chapters on creative philosophies (quoting many of the "big" names in advertising), copy, layout, print media, broadcast media, even Yellow Pages! An excellent book for students and practitioners alike.

Ogilvy, David. *Ogilvy on Advertising.* New York: Vintage Books, Random House, 1985. David Ogilvy is best known for the advertising campaigns his agency created, including the man with the eyepatch who wore a Hathaway shirt, Commander Whitehead for Schweppes, and the electric clock commercial for Rolls-Royce. This book provides insight into the world of advertising. The author describes advertising as a medium of information, not entertainment or an art form. His approach focuses on getting a return on investment—developing advertising that works, advertising that sells. An excellent book to help you relate advertising concepts to nonprofit organizations.

"We need to plan, develop, and execute promotion for our physicians. They are key to our marketing success. What can you do to promote them? If they succeed, we succeed!"

A Promotional Plan for Sharp HealthCare

That was the challenge posed to me and my colleagues by administrators and board members of Sharp HealthCare in San Diego, California. The logic was clear: If physicians using the health care system's facilities succeeded in attracting new patients (and keeping former patients), the system would benefit and thrive. Therefore, Sharp needed to promote these physicians.

As Sharp's director of marketing promotion, I was familiar with the problem. My experience with other nonprofits had revealed the same kind of challenges. How do you get internal target audiences to support your efforts to market? Other nonprofits, ranging from colleges and universities to symphony orchestras to hospitals, are in the same boat: If key internal (and often quite independent) service deliverers succeed, the sponsoring organization succeeds. But internal political pressures are often great. Internal groups (faculty, orchestral performers, physicians, and so on) cherish their independence. The challenge facing many nonprofit marketers is how to get important internal groups to participate in the organization's marketing efforts.

Sharp asked me to prepare promotion directed at two important target groups: patients who might use the health care system and physicians who might direct patients into the system.

Sharp had already put a lot of work into efforts to form an IPA (an Independent Physicians Association) composed of the best physicians in the San Diego county marketplace. A full-time consultant had been working for over a year to develop the organization. The physicians would serve as the primary medical referral base into Sharp HealthCare system's facilities. Sharp had also set up a physician referral telephone system, a computerized health care information system that would be operated by a customer service representative. Anyone could call a special number, 27-SHARP, to get information and referral and to make an appointment. Countless hours and many meetings had been spent on developing this idea.

Now I had the assignment of working with the organization's advertising agency to develop supporting promotion. My colleagues and I met with the creative staff of the agency to consider these points:

• How could we plan promotion to support Sharp physicians, reach key target markets, stay within a limited budget, and promote Sharp's services without appearing self-serving?

• How could we use research to create effective, return-on-investment promotion?

We decided that a 30-second television spot would be the best way to achieve our goals and objectives. Television, a medium that combines visual, oral, and written messages, provided great opportunities to tell the Sharp physicians' story in a short time. Television could also reach key target groups. It was expensive, but careful placement on cable as well as regular commercial channels could get the necessary viewer attention and spur him or her into action.

As we began to plan the spot, there were many problems. If the spot focused on Sharp physicians, how would we choose the doctors who would appear in it? Wouldn't those who weren't selected be offended? And what would the message be? The spot had to promote the physician referral service, but how could all the specialties provided by Sharp's complex, multi-location health care system be summarized in 30 seconds? And, even if this were possible, how could it be done within a limited budget?

After many meetings, involving many people (administrators, physicians, chief of the medical staff, agency creative people and media planners, board members, and advisory committee members) the solution emerged, and the spot began to take shape. We decided not to use real physicians but to hire actors. Since the budget was limited, videography would be done from black and white photographs of the physician-actors. All of the spot would be in black and white, except for the last frame which would display, in color, Sharp HealthCare's logo and the physician referral telephone number. We felt that the impact of black and white would be powerful on a medium that uses color almost exclusively, and we selected our photographer carefully. It was critical that photos not appear slick and staged. Actors, lighting, and action would have to be carefully controlled.

The final television spot was very simple, a series of "scenes" using videographic movement and dissolves recorded from black and white photo prints. Each scene included an actor portraying a Sharp physician. The "mix" of kinds of physicians subtly communicated the variety of health care services available at Sharp. Narration was very important, and the copy was simple but powerful:

Today, there are hundreds of Sharp physicians in San Diego County.

They come in all shapes and sizes.

There are generalists and specialists of every description.

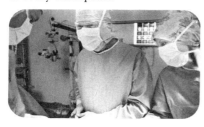

But as diverse as they are, you should know they share two things in common:

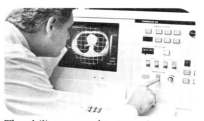

The ability to put the extensive research of Sharp HealthCare to work for you today

And the determination to make a difference.

The spot ended with Sharp's logo and the telephone number for the physician referral system.

We chose a narrator whose voice conveyed sincerity and professionalism. Music was created on a synthesizer. Sixteen tracks provided a "classical" but upbeat music bed that provided continuity. The same music was used for a 60-second companion radio spot.

The photographer did a masterful job. Actors suited up in scrub suits to observe an actual operation in order to get the feel of a real health care situation. We gave a lot of thought to the locations we used— operating rooms, doctors' offices, waiting rooms, and hospital hallways and lobbies. A quick review of the photographer's proof sheets revealed photos that were right on target. They looked and felt real.

I knew the promotional spot would be successful. We had covered all the bases. Careful work, based on market research and organizational knowledge, consumer wants and needs, media and promotional opportunities and limitations had produced an exciting solution. Only time (and evaluative market research) would tell just how successful it would be.

Worksheet 15

Planning and Executing Effective Marketing Promotion

1. Identify the service to be promoted.

2. What research is necessary to plan and execute this promotional activity?

3. Identify the target market(s).

4. Identify possible promotional "vehicles" (media).

5. List service aspects or positioning characteristics (as perceived from the target market's viewpoint) that should be considered.

6. What creative ideas emerge? Written? Visual? Audio? List them.

7. How will you promote your organization's overall umbrella image as related to specific services?

8. Plan a promotional time-line calendar. How do promotional efforts for different services relate to each other and to overall organizational efforts?

Chapter 12

Selecting Promotional Media: A Guide

E ach media vehicle has its advantages and disadvantages. For you, the marketing practitioner, selecting the proper media has important implications. One implication is cost. Some media are much more expensive than others. Another implication is effectiveness. Some media reach target markets more effectively than others.

It's your job to select media that match your marketing objectives within your promotion budget. The list below gives you some idea of the kinds of media available (you may discover other forms) and indicates the advantages and disadvantages of each.

Use this guide and Worksheet 16 at the end of this chapter to create a promotional plan that relates to your organization's marketing plan.

PRINT

NEWSPAPERS

Newspapers are a popular form of media for advertising nonprofits. Two promotional avenues are available to you through newspaper placement. One is free; the other requires paid space. Newspaper feature articles and news releases may result in free story placement for your nonprofit. Public relations efforts may yield results in getting stories, articles, or news items placed in a newspaper. Paid advertising is effective because you have total control of the message, and you can control placement by determining in what section of the newspaper the ad should run. Newspapers are important vehicles that enable you to reach the broad spectrum of your target audiences.

Advantages

- Metropolitan suburban papers offer intensive coverage (controlled saturation)
- Paid ads can by keyed to newspaper sections with specific editorial and reader focus (Arts, Education, Business, Editorial, Sports, Leisure, Food)
- Availability (in some instances) of geographical zoned editions
- Availability of inserts
- Can include detailed, complicated information
- Can include response mechanism (coupon)
- Date of publication, frequency, and reach are controlled
- Relatively low cost for saturation achieved
- Believability

Disadvantages

- Short life, soon discarded
- Reading is cursory, hasty
- Poor reproduction quality (inserts may be an exception)
- Selective reader exposure to different sections

MAGAZINES

Magazines have the advantage of reaching more specific target audiences than most newspapers. Because magazines are most often published about specific subjects, they reach specific target audiences. Magazines have a longer life than newspapers and often enjoy pass-along readership. You may want to consider magazines that focus on subjects relating to your nonprofit's area of subject matter and thereby offer excellent advertising opportunities to reach your organization's discrete target markets.

Advantages

- Target audience segmentation by interest
- Excellent reproduction potential
- Use of color
- Long life (increases secondary and tertiary exposure, good pass-along readership)
- Can include editorial detail and complex information
- Coupons can be used as response items

Disadvantages

- Requires longer production lead time
- Difficult to make last-minute changes
- Variation of timing (date) of reader exposure leads to lack of concentrated impact and planning
- Fewer opportunities for audience segmentation (depending on publication's ability to do regional runs)
- Often read hurriedly—results in selective exposure

DIRECT MAIL

Direct mail (sometimes called "direct marketing") is an excellent way to target promotional information to discrete target markets. Computerized mailing lists, which are becoming more and more sophisticated, can target your message to a good prospect. Direct mail encourages immediate action by asking the recipient to fill out a card or make a phone call. It also allows for recording, tracking, and analyzing so that you know exactly what works and what doesn't.

Advantages

- Extremely selective (ZIP code and carrier route)
- Pretesting can predict results
- Can build your own mailing lists segmented by target audience
- Can combine advertising with billing
- Excellent control over timing
- Flexible format, size, layout, graphics possible
- Computerized, personalized, customized messages
- Excellent editorial opportunity to control information and reminders in sequence to create reader interest
- Distribution costs an advantage (franking privilege)
- Can include response envelope (possibly prepaid for incentive, vehicle for check or reply)

Disadvantages

- High unit cost per addressee ($.50 to $1—can be less with very large runs)
- Dependency on mailing list accuracy
- Cost of updating computer mail lists
- Consumer resistance to "junk mail"
- Inability to control delivery date (especially for long distance, low rate mailings)

BROADCAST MEDIA

TELEVISION

Television provides wonderful opportunities for nonprofit promotion. It is a captivating medium that combines visuals, movement, and sound. Unfortunately, it is very expensive in two ways: production and placement. Good television spots are very expensive to produce. Television placement time is very expensive especially during prime time (times when the most people are viewing). But there is no denying that television is a powerful medium with great potential for dynamic impact.

Advantages

- Combines visuals, movement, and sound for high receiver impact
- Provides mass coverage

- Repetition (hourly, daily)
- Flexibility—wide variety of message format and content ("live" shots, stills, animation, computer graphics, color)
- Excellent audience research data are available
- "Big time" image (this may be a *disadvantage* for some types of nonprofit organizations)
- Timing of messages can be controlled and related to viewer numbers
- Message can relate to program content

Disadvantages

- High production cost
- Expensive (may not be if cable is used)
- Message is fleeting
- Lacks authenticity of print media
- Less easy to target markets in network programming (cable is easier)
- Short—message usually limited to 60 seconds or less
- Lacks narrow geographic focus

RADIO

Radio is an "imagination" medium. Sounds appeal to listeners' imagination. Radio provides wonderful opportunities to deliver strong messages. Radio targets very well—excellently, in fact. Most radio stations can provide excellent demographic information about their listeners. Your message can be targeted by the station you select to broadcast it. Your message can be read by an on-air announcer or you can provide a prerecorded audio tape.

Advantages

- Flexibility — can use any sound
- Less expensive (compared to TV)
- Short placement time (production not as complicated as TV)
- Excellent research data lead to excellent target audience segmentation by listenership demographics
- Can use foreign language and target to ethnic groups
- Highly mobile (cars, work, leisure)
- Quality (stereo FM and AM)
- Excellent time-of-day placement (for example, you can take advantage of "drive time"—mornings and early evenings when most people are driving to or from work)
- Good for short messages (reminders)

Disadvantages

- Very competitive (message can easily be "lost" in clutter)
- Fleeting message, less personal than TV

- Hard to communicate detailed, complicated information
- Difficult to focus on geographic areas

OTHER MEDIA

OUTDOOR BOARDS

Outdoor boards (billboards) in most areas provide good advertising exposure opportunities. Boards are available in two forms: painted and preprinted. Preprinted boards are made of many sheets that are pasted up to form one image. Boards are a good promotional medium because they provide repeat exposure. If you choose outdoor advertising, be very careful about location. Boards are like real estate—location is everything!

Advantages
- Location specific
- High repeat value (based on traffic patterns)
- Large size makes it easy to notice
- Can be used for long period of time
- Builds awareness and reinforces promotion

Disadvantages
- Many perceive as inferior medium
- May suggest unnecessary aggressiveness
- Requires very simple, short message
- No response mechanism
- May be prevented by local restrictions (visual pollution laws)

YELLOW PAGES

The Yellow Pages are, unfortunately, often overlooked by nonprofits. For many nonprofit service organizations, the Yellow Pages are one of the best forms of advertising from a cost efficiency and consumer usage point of view. They are limited in color (most often to two colors), but they get excellent distribution and enjoy a long life. Don't overlook the Yellow Pages as a viable advertising medium.

Advantages
- Widely distributed
- Long life span
- Used a lot

Disadvantages
- Expensive
- Limited in use of color
- Message must last for a long period of time and cannot be changed

POSTERS

Posters are relatively economical forms of advertising communication because they can be reproduced in large quantities with conventional printing equipment. Color, photography, typography, graphics, and illustration provide excellent communication opportunities.

Advantages

- No charge for placement
- Time and location specific
- Can include response item (return card)
- Low cost
- Can include visuals

Disadvantages

- Difficult to control readership
- Vulnerable to vandalism, theft
- If quality is poor, poster may communicate the idea of a low-budget, nonprofessional organization

SIGNAGE

Signage refers to permanent directional and informational signs. Signs allow opportunities to get your institution's name and logo out in front of the public on a permanent basis. Placement is free if signs are on your property. Signs are often overlooked by nonprofits as a possible advertising medium. Vehicles (cars, buses, trucks) also afford signage opportunities.

Advantages

- Provides permanent reminder
- Complements and reinforces personal or mass media messages
- Offers high exposure in high traffic areas
- Long lifetime—nighttime exposure
- Can be relatively inexpensive (compared to exposure value)

Disadvantages

- Complex information cannot be easily communicated
- Vulnerable to vandalism
- Maintenance costs
- Local restrictions may regulate placement, size, color, configuration, etc.
- Poor nighttime visibility (unless lighted)

Although originally written for higher education, this article provides "food for thought" for many nonprofits. With a few word changes, you can imagine this article applying to your nonprofit's service area or "business."

Customers Can't Kick Your Tires

Higher education's tires can't be kicked. Unlike hard products, higher education's services are, for the most part, intangible. The consumer cannot "kick your tires" to determine if the product is what he or she needs or expects.

How do people determine your service quality? Ever know anyone willing to sample an undergraduate degree? Or some graduate study? Or an alumni event or two? Some food service? Wait in the parking permit line? Or execute a research project to determine if your quality levels are up to expectations?

Judging the quality of your services

How *do* users judge the quality of higher education's services? Word of mouth? Family networking? Checking your latest accreditation? Checking membership in professional organizations? Talking to your administrators, faculty, students, parents, donors?

The truth of the matter is that people have very few ways to check the quality of your institution's services. They almost never know if the professor used the right manuals or if the lab equipment is up-to-date. They don't know if the faculty member delivering instruction is credentialed or not. They base their feelings on *trust*.

How to build trust

How can you make sure that the idea of trust and the perceptions of quality are understood by all your target audiences, internal and external? How can you make sure that your institution is always perceived as possessing the kind of attributes you want people to relate to it? How can you be sure they will associate your name with quality and have trust in your "products"?

Higher education has become a business—a very competitive business. It's a business that is forced to identify target audiences that are important to survival and growth—counselors, faculty, parents, alumni, donors, media representatives, board members, corporate leaders, business people, family members, friends, department leaders, support staff, administrators. The list goes on and on.

How can your institution convey ideas of quality to achieve trust from all the people that are important to you? What tools do you have available to engender this critical idea? How can you make sure it's working?

People have "images" of your organization and its service components in their minds. They have images of your competitors as well.

Build a positive image

How can you make sure that your organization has the kind of image you want it to have? An image based on the quality you want to be known for? The answer is simple—*communications.* Communications based on the service areas you are known for; communications that have direct relationship to the business plan and marketing activities you execute; communications that support many ventures, including admissions, fund raising, and philanthropy.

Whose job is it to make sure that the proper communications are developed and delivered to key target audiences in order to constantly repeat and support ideas of quality; communications that will support your marketing, outreach, and business development efforts; communications that will solve problems, not create them?

A great part of this burden of communicating your institution to constituencies is assumed by the people who do public relations and marketing. It is their job to apply all the skills they have to make sure that important ideas are communicated. They use words, photos, images, production ideas, distribution. They combine these concepts with knowledge about marketing, public relations, development, direct mail, advertising, media placement, institutional advancement, promotion.

Every day there are people talking about your institution. Ideally, you stimulate many of those conversations. You feed ideas to many publics about your services. You position your services among those of your competitors. You try to make sure that your customers, even though they can't kick your tires, are left with feelings of quality that build trust.

How do you do it?

Promotional information in the form of brochures, booklets, newsletters, advertisements, direct mail, and many other forms of media combine with information and news you place in the press and on television. Your objective is to get your organization's name and its services out in the marketplace, so when someone thinks of quality education they think of you. Look for every opportunity to get your name out to the public. Your public comprises many groups of segmented audiences. Make sure a group receives carefully targeted information based on what will influence that group in positive ways. Try to "speak" to that group in ways the group will understand. Use market research to understand how that group feels about you and to find out what you could do to get better results by improving their perceptions.

Worth a thousand words

Visuals (photographs, pictures, film images, television) play an important part in the way you position your organization in the competitive marketplace. Use a lot of pictures of people. Avoid equipment, buildings, and dull shots of unimportant things. Instead, use pictures of people—people helping people. Try to capture those emotional moments that are so common to quality education. Higher education is a series of unfolding experiences. Find ways to capture that excitement. Show faculty—lots of faculty at work, striving to help their students. It's an emotional story. Every day there are hundreds of emotional dramas taking place within your system. Try to capture some of that drama in words and pictures and deliver them into the marketplace to influence people. Influence them with fact and reality about your quality educational services.

The power of the word

"Marry" visuals with words—words that are carefully written to do justice to the people you represent. The power of words is a tool that you can use very effectively. The *way* you write is important. But the words and ideas are most important to your audience, the people to whom you are communicating. Try to find the best ways to deliver those ideas, words, and pictures through media. Forms of media are the "vehicles" that carry your messages out into the marketplace. Put these marketing communications techniques together to position your organization in the competitive higher education marketplace. Be careful to make sure that your messages are distinct and clear, that they focus the viewers' and readers' attention on the fact that your institution is a *quality* organization, one that has earned their *trust*.

Graphic continuity

Graphics are important to the way your institution is perceived. Every time your institution's name appears in public, it is important that it be recognized and associated with all the powerful quality ideas that you are trying to communicate. Outreach items must look and feel consistent, clean, organized, planned, methodical. There's no place for materials that look or feel dirty, haphazard, unplanned, or uncontrolled. Those negative ideas suggest that your institution is not as good as you want it to be and others expect it to be. Simple items such as typography, color, printing specifications, and layout are very important.

You may have earned a strong place in the marketplace. Faculty, students, administrators, board members, and support employees may have worked hard to help position your institution in the marketplace. The public has donated time and money. It is your responsibility to make sure that that position remains strong and permanent.

Yes. Customers can't kick your tires. But your college, school, or university will be at top-of-mind when people think of quality higher education. If you have done your marketing job well, you have earned their trust.

Reprinted from Marketing Higher Education, *a newsletter produced by Topor & Associates, Marketing and Communications Consulting for Nonprofit Organizations.*

101

Worksheet 16

Planning Promotional Media

Product name (service(s) to be promoted):

_____

_____

_____

Target audience(s):

_____

_____

_____

Budget planner:

Production cost plus insertion cost times number of insertions equals promotion costs.

_____

_____

_____

Exposure planner:

Potential media reach (number of people) times number of insertions equals total number of target audience reached.

_____

_____

_____

Timing calendar:

Plan a calendar to coordinate promotional activities for services and "umbrella" organization-wide promotional activities. Plan so that promotions for specific product lines (groups of services) are coordinated. Remember that timing is critical, and don't overlook other factors that may determine the best timing (seasonal, competitive, media costs).

_____

_____

_____

Chapter 13

Creating Print Advertising

It isn't easy to advertise nonprofit "products" (services). They're difficult to quantify, tough to photograph, and hard to describe. Consider for a moment how you would advertise higher education. What is it? What are its services? How can you describe them in promotional copy?

An organization for health care has the same problem. How does it promote health? What is it "selling"? Who are the customers—referral physicians, the patient, third-party groups buying health care insurance, the patient's family? Should a symphony orchestra promote its performances as entertainment, education, or social activity?

These difficult questions have no easy answers, and the traditional nonprofit environment only makes the situation worse. By its nature, the nonprofit environment is not advertising oriented. In fact, for many such organizations, the very idea of advertising runs against the grain. Nevertheless, for most nonprofits, advertising has become a reality.

Inflation, reduced budgets, changing demographics, and increased competition for customers and resources have forced many nonprofit organizations to consider advertising.

Advertising is a serious business. It is not art for art's sake, nor writing for the sake of writing. It is not exposure for the purpose of exposure only. It should *do* something. Successful advertising is direct and action oriented. It is closer to "hard sell" than to passive, informational communication. It is persuasive, concise, and focused. It should convince the reader. It should motivate.

To succeed, advertising must be clear and consistent. Contradictions confuse. Discrepancies blur perceptions and images.

Human beings tend toward inertia. It's always easier to continue doing what you've been doing than to change. Change makes people nervous. Reproducing past efforts is safe, comfortable, easy. We all know that new ideas are often not as good as old ones, and we try to forget that sometimes they're better! Successful advertisers don't fear new ideas. They thrive on them. You should too.

Nonprofit organizations live in competitive times. They must seize every opportunity for organizational advancement. Advertising is one such opportunity. Use it wisely.

There are as many ways to strategize, write, design, and place advertisements as there are creative people to produce them. The information that follows attempts to describe some of these ideas and how they can be adapted to nonprofit organizations. Use this chapter and Worksheet 17 as practical guides to assist you in planning, writing, and executing print advertising for your organization. Share this chapter with others on your marketing team. These ideas represent many years of practical experience and many successes tempered by many failures, but remember that they are just ideas, not rules: Think of them as suggestions, not formulas.

What follows are the major elements to consider as you create an advertisement.

Context

While you want your customers (target markets) to remember what you're advertising, first you want them to relate your services to your organization and its service category—that is, what your organization does. Existing services and recognizable identities are the framework in which advertising endeavors to place a new product in the consumer's mind. The reader must perceive the service in the context of familiar ideas.

If you are advertising a service of a university or college, first introduce the concept of education, then the idea of your institution, and finally introduce your service.

A hospital should present the key idea of health care, then the institution, and then the particular service.

A symphony orchestra should focus on the concept of music, then the orchestra, and finally the event being advertised and the particular pieces and musicians on the program.

It's important that you include all of these levels of information. Each supports the others. Without them, your ad may "self-destruct" because it's too fragmented for the consumer to grasp readily. In other words, your ad must clearly communicate vital information about your service category, your organization, and its specific services.

Once you present your service in terms of this natural framework, you then try to make it stand out in that arena. When all services in a field are basically similar, focus attention on comparative differentiation, that is, the idea that your service somehow stands apart from similar, competing services. For example, create memorable personalities that will stand out in the audience's mind and memory. These personalities should represent what people want or need.

Appeal

The appeal is the reason your reader will have positive perceptions about your non-profit organization and its services. The appeal is critical. It's more important than the manner in which it's presented; with apologies to Marshall McLuhan, the medium is *not* the message. The *appeal* is the message!

Here are some appeals that work:
- Save money.
- Make more money.
- Lose weight.
- End drudgery.
- Have more leisure time.
- Attain better health.
- Become more comfortable.
- Gain freedom from worry.
- Become more secure.
- Get a degree.
- Get a job.
- Advance in your career.
- Avoid embarrassment.

List some appeals you could use for your organization's services. Your readers should discover benefits and responses to their needs and wants in your ads.

Once you've identified your organization's appeals, you need to repeat them, saying the same thing in different ways. For example, a hospital might use key words such as "healthful," "well-being," "preventive," "quality," "caring," and "responsive."

Remember, advertisements that involve your reader are better than those that do not. Active is better than passive. Your headline, copy, and illustration can achieve this. For example, you might use an engaging photo or illustration, stimulating body copy, or a headline that poses a question.

Avoid trendy ideas in favor of simple, plain-Jane, everyday concepts. People may interpret a "cutesy" ad in two ways—they may notice and remember the ad but reject its gimmicks when they are making a decision about your services.

Test your ads. Find out what works and why and what doesn't work and why. Ads that win awards are not necessarily the ones that work best.

Content

Your most difficult decisions involve the content of your ad. What should you say? To whom? Why? Here are some ideas that may help you determine content:
- Think of your ad in terms of your target market.
- Describe the problem your service answers.
- Give promises of solutions.
- Explain the promises or answers.
- Give proof of the solutions.

- Give a reason for the reader to respond actively.
- Provide a response mechanism (coupon, phone number, and so forth).
- Remember your reader's wants and needs.

You can think of these ideas as ways to accomplish the following five steps:

1. Get attention.
2. Arouse interest.
3. Provide solutions.
4. Stimulate desire.
5. Get an action response.

Your organization's service should be center stage. It's the star of the ad. But unless the ad relates the service to the reader's wants and needs, he or she won't remember either your nonprofit or its services.

Readers of your advertisement have two opposing forces at work in their minds: skepticism and the desire to believe. Truth in advertising encourages belief. It will increase response. Untruths (even the suggestion of falsehood) will encourage skepticism. Specific statements are more believable than generalities. Testimonials, particularly those attributed to people with whom your target audience can relate, are effective. People believe other people more than they believe you. (You have a vested interest, after all.)

Straightforward is better than circuitous. You can plan and execute an effective advertising campaign around a simple, direct idea. Present your message as a theme and variations on a theme.

Writing

Enthusiasm counts. We all like an enthusiastic presentation. In advertising, as in sales, the enthusiastic presentation wins acceptance.

To write enthusiastic copy, think enthusiastically. Write fast. Pretend you're writing to a friend or neighbor, and don't let inhibitions or doubts slow you down. Pour it out—write down those wild, persuasive, energetic thoughts. Let your ideas flow. You can boil them down later.

Push criticism and negativism out of your mind. Negative thoughts will only drain away the juices of creativity. Write with enjoyment and passion. Don't let "musts" and "can'ts" into your mind. Remember that someone once said how-to-do-it manuals are for adolescent lovers and would-be plumbers.

Get fired up. You can't pump life into dead copy, but you can tone down passionate writing later.

Gather more information than you need, then boil it down to its simplest form. You're aiming for precise, fact-filled, benefits-oriented copy.

Your creative mental process goes on all the time, everywhere. One way to improve an ad is to leave it alone for a day or so and then go back and rework it. You will find it easier to add new ideas and to edit old copy.

Style

Let's look at some methods that will increase the effectiveness of your ad copy.

Use the present tense and the second person. Describe your service as if the reader has already subscribed to it. Rather than "you will," use "you are."

Use simple words. Be direct. Several short, simple words are better than one long complicated one. Use a simple writing style. Easier is better. Don't expect lots of time and energy from your readers. You won't get it. Avoid long sentences and paragraphs. Make your ad ideas easily digestible.

Avoid unnecessary words. Edit. Edit. Edit. Most copy improves with cutting. Count the words Lincoln used in the Gettysburg Address and see if you can add any to make it better (you can't!).

Use action verbs. Use concrete terms that evoke a picture in the reader's mind. Build on the reader's experience. Relate your ideas to the reader's.

Use understated copy. Overstating invites skepticism. No one likes a braggart.

Make ads informative. Give free information. Build interest with facts, specifics, and useful information. Be specific. It is better to say, "4,938 babies were born at Providence Hospital last year" than to say, "Nearly 5,000 babies were born...."

Don't be afraid of long copy. Readership surveys show that people will read long copy if it's interesting, benefits-oriented, and truthful. Direct marketing advertisers have found that long copy sells more.

Use subheads. Subheads can break up long, uninviting copy. Subheads can tell your story at a glance. In that respect, they are similar to well-written photo captions. The best ads communicate successfully at different levels: head, subhead, photo, logo, and body copy.

The best way to kill a bad product is to advertise it. No amount of advertising will sell a bad product. If you think you have a bad product or service, your time and money would be much better spent on improving that particular product than on advertising it.

Have you noticed that I have been using advertising copy style in this chapter? I could have written this chapter using all sorts of complicated, theory-based, obscure, esoteric, jargon-loaded copy. Wouldn't that have turned you off?

Text

The text of your advertisement breaks down into component parts—headline, subheads, lead copy, and body copy.

Headline. The most important part of an ad is the headline. Headlines reach out and grab your readers. The best way to compel your readers' attention is to appeal to their self-interest.

Every headline should do at least one of the following:

- Appeal to the reader's self-interest.
- Have news value.
- Offer a way to solve a problem.
- Appeal to the reader's curiosity; this one can't work by itself but it can be powerful when combined with self-interest.

Simple language is best. The best head communicates a complex idea in simple terms. Remember Volkswagen's "Think Small," Avis's "We try harder," 7-Up's "The Un-Cola."

How much time do you have to get your reader's attention? A few seconds at best. Make that time work for you. Don't waste it by being vague, mysterious, confusing, or cute. Avoid gloomy or negative heads. Be positive and optimistic.

But don't make your headline short at the expense of communicating your idea. A long headline that says something is better than a short headline that doesn't.

What would make *you* read the headline and consider the service it promotes? The reader is not an abstraction or a crowd. Think of the reader as an individual representing the target market—not one of a faceless crowd.

Suggest a convenient way for readers to get what they want and need. Write believable heads (avoid *National Enquirer*-style heads). Curiosity by itself is weak as a motivating factor.

Don't write "dead" heads—heads that just sit there and communicate little or nothing. Don't write literary works. Don't try to be smart, cute, or artsy.

Consider your logo in context with your head. Whether your logo appears at the top or the bottom of your ad, it should work with and not against the head.

Type size and style (roman, bold, italic, caps, small caps) can emphasize important words and ideas.

Here are some ideas to help you create a dynamic headline:

- *Immediacy grabs.* Use important first words: "Announcing..." "Introducing..." "Presenting..." "New..." "Free..." "At last..." "Beginning soon...."
- *Use news writing style.* This straightforward approach will make your copy sound more believable: "The course to help your career advancement" or "Quality health care at a convenient location."
- *Offer valuable information.* "Osteoporosis threatens one out of every four women."
- *Begin with "how to."* "How to lose inches in a few weeks."
- *Begin with "why."* "Why you suffer from migraine headaches." "Why collecting antiques is profitable."
- *Begin with "which."* "Which computer is best for you?" "Which personality problems would you like to correct?"
- *Begin with "this."* "This new course in marketing will help you...." "This is the time to...."
- *Offer advice.* "Advice to college dropouts." "Advice to new mothers."
- *Offer a challenge or test.* "Could you climb a mountain?" "How happy are you in your job?"
- *Use price-oriented information.* "What does $12,000 of tuition buy?"
- *Offer specials.* "New subscribers receive one-third off the newsstand price."

- *Feature something free.* "All season ticket holders will receive a free cassette of the concert of their choice."
- *Use a testimonial.* "'I never thought I could finish college,' says Bob Johnson."
- *Use only one word.* "Education." "Health." "Success." "Learning."
- *Use only two words.* "Higher education." "Your health." "Success? Yes." "Convenient learning."
- *Call upon experts.* Let an official (your university president, health care organization CEO, or orchestra or museum director) speak in your headline.
- *Address a specific target audience and write in their language.* "Do you hanker for Haydn? Does your heart beat for Beethoven?"
- *Tell a story.* "How I made a million dollars in real estate."

Subheads. Consider what a subhead can do to grab the reader's attention. My favorite source for headline, subhead, and lead writing techniques is the *Reader's Digest.* A recent article about the space shuttle tragedy was titled "CHALLENGER." The subhead was "Reflections on a Tragedy."

Lead copy. Besides headlines and subheads, the next most important editorial component is the lead copy. Again, *Reader's Digest* excels. The Challenger article began as follows:

> *Cocoa Beach, Fla:* T minus 6 hours, 8 minutes and counting. As I stepped onto the balcony of my hotel room, an icy wind hit me, unlike anything I had encountered in covering 11 space-shuttle flights.

That's copy that pulls you into the article. Ad lead copy should do the same. It should entice the reader into reading further.

Many writers start with a preamble, overview, or introductory copy. That approach is suitable for constitutions but not for advertising copy. It will kill reader interest. Edit your copy critically. You may find that your real ad starts at the second or third paragraph.

Carry through the headline idea without repeating it in the same words. Let lead copy explore the headline idea or use a "breaker," an idea that shocks the reader. Some Madison Avenue people call this the "fish in the face" approach. A famous headline for a body-building ad was, "Don't get sand kicked in your face." Don't be afraid to surprise the reader or to present unusual thoughts and ideas.

Tie your head, subheads, and lead copy together by using the same facts and specifics, similar adjectives, and several different ways of arousing curiosity about the subject.

Your lead copy should follow these three basic rules:

1. Practice brevity (don't discourage readers before they begin).
2. Continue the head/subhead ideas.
3. State consumer-oriented benefits ("What's in it for me?").

Body copy. The body copy—that is, the rest of the ad—should embody the same qualities as the head, subheads, and lead copy. Analyze the body copy of your ad by answering the following questions:

- Does it tell readers how the service will satisfy their goals, needs, and wants?

- Is it interesting to a prospective user?
- Is it accurate?
- Is it clear?
- Is it factual?
- Does it provide adequate information?
- Is it plausible?
- Will it appeal to a reader?
- Does it hold reader attention?

Layout and design

Writing the ad is one thing. Creating an appropriate and compelling layout is another. The best ads occur when writer and designer work together; one concept adds to the other without discord or conflict.

Like a good headline, layout, graphic design, typography, and reproduction should attract and hold reader attention. Again, simplicity and directness are called for—don't use hidden, hard-to-understand "art" concepts. Be distinctive, but not at the expense of clarity. The layout could be inconspicuous and still highlight the basic message.

Analyze your layout by answering the following questions:
- Does it quickly communicate ideas of interest to your reader?
- Does it support editorial concepts?
- Does it make the ad accessible? Easy to read and understand?
- Does the main idea get main attention?
- Can anything be removed without impairing the message?
- Does it leave the desired impression?
- Is critical identity evident? That is, is your organization appropriately identified?
- How does your ad stack up against competing ads?

The designer must forget "art for art's sake" just as the writer must forget literary writing. Advertising design can be fine art, but not at the expense of effective communication and results.

Typography. Type is the designer's tool for presenting words and ideas. Type should be easy to read. Avoid intricate typefaces. Avoid using a lot of italics. Avoid type that speaks about itself at the expense of your message. Avoid type in reverse (white type on a black background). Avoid printing type over photos or illustrations—the result makes both type and photo difficult to comprehend. My Syracuse University professor of journalism was adamant: "Type is meant to be read." He was right.

Type size is important. It suggests attention to hierarchy, a comprehension of the importance of things. Sometimes it's good to shout. At other times a whisper may be called for. It all depends on the situation. Consider type size in terms of your target audience. Older people like large type that is easy to read.

White space is important. Designers know that the eye and mind need "rests" from active elements. Just as in music, sometimes what you don't see (or hear) is as important—or more important—than what you do see. Don't be afraid to use white space.

If you write a long headline, tell the designer which words are key. If you're the designer, ask the writer to identify key words and ideas.

Illustrations. High pictorial value does not necessarily mean high ad value. The most effective ad illustrations show the advertised service being used. They communicate the benefits of using the service, and they encourage viewers to project themselves into the ad.

Readership studies have shown that certain visuals get high readership attention:

- animals;
- babies;
- brides;
- famous people;
- people in unusual costumes;
- romantic pictures;
- pictures that tell a story;
- pictures of people in unusual situations;
- catastrophes; and
- news pictures.

In general, men tend to look at ads showing men while women look at ads showing women.

Evidence shows that photos generally score better than artwork with viewers. Photos are more believable, more immediate. A quick look at a photo is almost as good as seeing the real thing. One of the best ways to get attention is to use a photo of a person who appears to be looking straight at the reader. Testimonials gain value if accompanied by a photo of the person endorsing the service—especially if his or her attention appears to be riveted on the reader.

Remember, there are no hard-and-fast rules. Some ads work best with no illustration, photo, or visual (graphic elements).

Placement

Now that you have created your advertisement, you must decide where it should appear. The best conceived, written, designed, and produced ad will fall short of expectations if it's not seen by the right people and the right target audience. Placement is critical. Chapter 12 can help you select the appropriate promotional media.

Before you select your advertising vehicle, you must determine where you want your ad to go and to whom. You may be looking for a wide distribution or hoping to reach a small but select group. Determine how many readers you want to reach and what kind. For example, do you want your ad to appear in a publication that is hand-delivered or distributed free and hung on doorknobs?

There are many print vehicles available. Many cities have newspapers that print morning and evening editions, each with different readership and different attributes. Local community papers, pennysavers or shopping guides, and special interest newspapers (women's papers, business papers, student papers) all have their own audiences. Magazines, like newspapers, appeal to different audiences.

Money is always a concern, especially for nonprofits. Large metropolitan newspapers charge more for advertising space than small, local papers. But you need to balance the cost against the readership. The cost is greater for a cheap ad that nobody sees than for a relatively expensive insertion in the publication many of your customers and potential customers read. How many times you run the ad and how big it is will determine cost.

Decide how often your ad will run and at what time intervals. To be effective, ads must run several times to build up recognition. Ads that are scheduled to run over a period of time are called "flights." You should plan flights carefully so that they will achieve the best results.

Advertising is important. It is your window to the world. It's the way many target audiences get to know about your organization and its services. But please don't do advertising just for the sake of doing advertising! Do advertising to achieve measurable marketing results.

Norman A. Darais is director of publications for Brigham Young University in Provo, Utah. A writer who works closely with graphic designers, Darais describes how this process helps to create successful marketing materials.

Achieving Harmony: The Graphic Art

The best graphic art projects a pervasive sense of harmony, however subtle. Once the idea, concept, or flash of inspiration arrives, the challenge becomes one of selection and organization—choosing the most forceful visual and verbal elements and harmoniously ordering, or designing, them in the most captivating way.

Successful graphic communications integrate words and images so skillfully that the organizing sense of harmony often becomes a rather subdued, if not an almost invisible, element. But it is there, nevertheless, and its cohesive effect is vital.

How is this harmony achieved? Ideally, it's a matter of a highly compatible writer, designer, and photographer or illustrator working to achieve a common purpose. Each is a specialist. Each builds and enhances the graphic statement. There must be no preconceived notions, no sacred ways, no traditional starting points.

As a writer I enjoy—and even anticipate—a freewheeling flexibility, an unpredictability, in the creative people I work with.

Therefore, when working with designs and images, I too must be flexible—always willing to bend and blend. The text doesn't necessarily come first. Sometimes a photograph or the design itself may give rise to the words or their shape. I may shorten copy, lengthen it, change it, rearrange it—even work with specific key words or initial letters—to make it more unified, more congruent with the graphics.

When words and images are successfully synthesized into the ultimate form, a synergistic harmony is achieved. Images acknowledge and build upon words. Words enhance images. The result is an enticing, compelling graphic communication.

Worksheet 17

Elements of Print Advertising

Use this worksheet to help consider the important elements as you plan your advertisement.

H E A D L I N E

_____

S U B H E A D
(the "bridge" between the headline and the body copy)

_____

I L L U S T R A T I O N
(if you choose to use one—or more)

_____

L E A D C O P Y
(an important part of your advertisement)

_____

_____

_____

B O D Y C O P Y

_____

_____

Subhead: _____

_____

_____

_____

Subhead: _____

_____

_____

_____

_____

_____

_____

C O U P O N
(response mechanism)

_____

_____

_____

L O G O
Slogan (if you choose to use one)
Name of organization
Address, phone number

Chapter 14

Using Sales as Part of Your Total Marketing Effort

Nonprofit organizations today find themselves part of a complex and highly competitive environment. A nonprofit organization can no longer assume it has an automatic, ready-made market. Its potential users have wider choices than ever before, often including similar services provided by for-profit organizations. In many cases, the nonprofit could greatly benefit by using direct sales techniques. But most nonprofits, even those that have been quick to develop marketing functions, have been reluctant to use direct sales techniques.

A for-profit business, on the other hand, usually chooses sales as one of the first marketing tools when it has developed a new product or service. For business, sales are a must to generate cash flow for growth and development. But many nonprofits are unfamiliar with (and therefore skeptical about) the sales function. Many nonprofits don't know how to set up a sales organization; they don't understand the kinds of benefits sales can bring in terms of consumer feedback that contains vital marketing information.

Often even those nonprofits that use sales do not do it properly; they do not coordinate and plan the sales effort as part of the total marketing process.

It's important to recognize that nonprofit organizations *do* participate in sales activities whether they admit it or not. They have sales people on their staffs but call them admissions representatives, development officers, outreach coordinators, or field representatives. So the use of sales, for nonprofits, is not a new idea.

You can think of your nonprofit as the operator of many small businesses. Each business has its own target markets, and you must actively sell your services to each target market. This calls for a well-planned and well-managed direct sales effort.

How to promote a sales concept

For most nonprofits the concept of actively selling services is not only foreign, but includes negative stereotypes of aggressive and often obnoxious salespeople.

But sales can be a positive force when the nonprofit develops sales as a consultative, educational effort to build a long-term relationship with the target market. For example, a health care organization may employ a person to promote educational assistance programs targeted at corporations. These efforts may focus on "selling" alcohol and drug screenings or use of emergency centers for occupational health services.

For a college or university, an outreach "sales" person might work to establish relationships with corporations to contract for bioengineering research services.

This approach provides client-oriented, sensitive outreach. To develop consultative sales, you need to:
- determine the target market's needs, wants, or problems;
- determine how your services can help answer the target market's needs; and
- establish long-term relationships, oriented to problem solving through education, with focus on the target market's environment.

These are important concepts to consider as you plan to establish consultative, educational sales activities.

Creating, establishing, and maintaining a sales function

The process of creating, establishing, and maintaining a sales function can be broken down into three steps: defining sales, organizing sales as part of your marketing process, and managing the sales function.

Step 1: Defining sales. Before you begin this step, you should consider the role of sales in your nonprofit organization, the difference between selling services and selling tangible products, and the types of direct sales techniques that will be acceptable to your organization.

Nonprofits have traditionally focused inward. But sales are driven by an outwardly directed focus, just as marketing is. Sales are one of the key elements of marketing for a nonprofit organization. (The others are market research, management of services, public relations, advertising, and promotion.)

Market research and management of services are planning functions, but public relations, advertising, and sales are "persuasion functions" that consist of communication with target markets. These persuasion functions form the bridge between your organization and the outside world of your target markets.

Sales differ from public relations and advertising in the following ways:
- Sales are personal in nature, resulting in the formation of a consultative bond with the target market.
- Sales are long term in focus; they build strong and enduring relationships.
- Sales are targeted to specific members of your audience.
- Sales are directed to your nonprofit organization's users through one-on-one personal contact.

Sales personnel can supply your organization with important information about competitors, customers' reaction to services, and marketplace trends and changes.

It is important to recognize the differences between selling your services and selling soap. The chart below shows some of these differences:

Tangible product	Nonprofit service
Product is tangible	Service is usually intangible
Seller can demonstrate the product	Seller must prove service's value through user's experience
Product has rigid design	Service can be customized
Product has easy-to-measure costs	Service's actual costs are hard to determine
Product quality can be tested and seen	Service quality is perceived "image"
Product has standard replacement parts with guarantees/warranties	If service "fails," seller may have to replace entire program
Product can be pretested and tried out	Service can be observed in action; testing may require that salesperson set up special test for user's review
Seller can benefit from economies of scale through mass production and volume	Economies of scale are difficult to obtain

Sales techniques for nonprofits

Many nonprofits attempt to use the high quality of their services as a selling point. But when services are intangible, there is often no tangible evidence of quality. And quality is difficult to sell anyway. It is extremely difficult to establish a comparative differential advantage based on the abstract idea of quality. Users need more concrete reasons to "buy" your product.

Many factors go into your users' perception of the quality of your services. These include:

- users' past experience with a similar service;
- users' past experience with your organization;
- image of your organization (based on word-of-mouth, public relations, advertising, facilities, and so on);
- testimonials and references;

- comparison of your services to competitors' services;
- users' ability to satisfy their needs and wants elsewhere;
- users' knowledge and understanding of your services;
- users' perception of your nonprofit and what it can do to satisfy their needs and wants;
- users' perception of the value provided by your services; and
- users' perception of your salesperson (professionalism, knowledge, personality, credibility, follow-up, and so on).

If you hope to use the quality and value of your service as a selling point, you must first find out how your target market evaluates quality and value. Then you need to design your services to meet these perceived characteristics and use marketing to reinforce their perception.

Your sales goals should be customer problem solving, customer education, service, relationship building, and referral to other services provided by your nonprofit.

Step 2: Organizing sales as part of your marketing process. Use Worksheet 18 at the end of this chapter to collect information about your organization's current sales efforts—if any. Then determine the total sales efforts for your organization. Identify any gaps that may provide special marketing opportunities. You will need to determine what to sell and to whom to sell it. Once you have identified your market, you will need to segment it into target markets.

Step 3: Managing the nonprofit sales function includes planning, implementing, and monitoring the sales effort. Few nonprofits have sales management functions in place. As a result, their sales activities are neither coordinated nor managed. As sales efforts expand, sales management becomes essential. The following elements are critical to the successful sales effort:

- Account research: You need to plan and execute account research to determine successes, shortcomings, and opportunities for the sales effort.
- Forecasting: Predicting sales enables your organization to plan for the future.
- Hiring, motivating, and training salespeople: Credibility for sales depends heavily on the personalities and the demeanor of the people representing your organization.
- Tracking success and monitoring sales performance: Evaluation and feedback are keys to successful sales management.

Nonprofits need to move from passive attitudes about outreach sales to active sales efforts. Proactive sales suggest concentrated aggressive efforts to reach out to target markets.

For many nonprofits, successful integration of proactive sales into the marketing mix will become more and more important. Nonprofits must accept sales as a tool that can be applied to achieve institutional goals and objectives without threatening the organization's integrity. It is part of your job to assess your nonprofit and its services to determine sales opportunities; to coordinate, expand, and manage the sales effort to serve your target market's wants and needs; and to prove—by acquiring new users and retaining old ones—that sales can be successfully integrated into nonprofit marketing.

Worksheet 18

Assessing Your Organization's Current Sales Efforts

Use this questionnaire to evaluate current sales efforts and plan future efforts.

1. Name of service:

_____

_____

2. Description:

_____

_____

3. Department or area overseeing this sales effort:

_____

_____

4. Type of sales efforts used (telephone, direct personal calls, direct mail, etc.):

_____

_____

_____

_____

5. Target markets:

_____

_____

6. Names and titles of people involved in sales efforts:

_____

_____

_____

_____

Section 4

The Marketing Planning Map: A Marketing Blueprint

Chapter 15

Exploring the Marketing Planning Map

There's much truth to that old Chinese saying, "The longest journey begins with one small step." When you are attempting to market a nonprofit organization, the journey seems long and complicated at first with many roadblocks such as traditional distrust of marketing, fear of new ideas, the complexities of the political environment, suspicious colleagues, difficulties of funding, and various misunderstandings.

You may be intimidated before you start. But if you use the marketing planning map (Figure 13 on the next page), you can plan a safe and comfortable journey that avoids some of the potholes, traffic jams, and roadblocks on the marketing road. The marketing planning map is the guide to developing your organization's marketing plan. This is where all the marketing ideas you have studied in this guidebook come together.

At first the map may look confusing. There's a lot going on; it's complicated. But nonprofit organizations *are* complicated. That's why this map is so important. It can help you simplify the complex marketing task by breaking it down into simple steps, just as the long journey begins with one simple step.

Examining internal forces

Now look at the marketing planning map. The first thing you will notice is that the map "starts" at the left, with external forces. It does *not* start with your organization. This brings us back to something I've discussed several times in this book: the tendency of nonprofits to navel-gaze, to look at themselves from the inside out rather than from the outside in. Traditionally, nonprofit organizations have focused on themselves—on program development, budgeting, funding, personnel, admin-

126

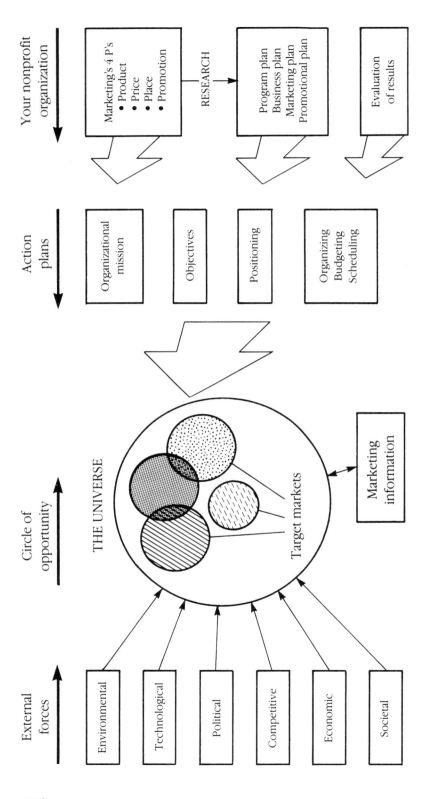

Figure 13: Marketing Planning Map

istration, resource development, program review, program research, teaching, and so on. Rarely have they examined external forces.

At first they didn't need to. Funding, in the form of gift income and appropriations, was not a problem in the past. The public saw nonprofits as necessary, fundamental, and good. Few questions were asked; few criticisms raised. Fiscal support, in many cases, was automatic. Hospitals enjoyed ever-growing cost reimbursement and public funding. Bond issues to support new ventures and new buildings were easily passed. Colleges and universities enjoyed steady increases in support. The number of students who wanted to attend college kept growing. Symphony orchestras and theater companies flourished. Zoos received funds for expansion and new facilities. Nonprofits thrived. The kinds of pressures now facing nonprofits did not exist. It was logical, in this kind of environment, for nonprofit organizations to pay more attention to what they were doing than to the world around them.

Then came the inevitable—big changes in many societal, economic, political, technological, competitive, demographic, and perceptional forces, and all at the same time. For most nonprofits, these changes were radical and painful, made all the worse because they were, in most cases, unanticipated and stressful.

Faced with these new forces, nonprofits that continue to look inward will face "ratcheting down" (cutting staff and budgets), program elimination, and more serious threats of consolidation, absorption by competitive profit-making organizations, or closure.

Organizations that hope to survive need to understand the new environment and determine how the organization should change. That's why the marketing planning map begins with external forces. Ask yourself some important questions:

- Why am I here?
- Why is my organization here?
- What external forces are important to my organization?
- Where must I direct my attention?
- What opportunities are available? What limitations?
- And, most importantly, how can marketing work for me and my organization? How do I proceed?

The marketing planning map can help you answer these questions. Let's begin by analyzing the following external forces as they affect your organization.

Environmental forces: trends, developments, conditions, events, and processes that influence—or may influence—your nonprofit organization. Environmental forces may be direct (such as federal funding) or indirect (such as laws that relate to one of your target markets). These external forces affect external groups or individuals (markets, competition, key audiences) as well as the internal organization itself (programs, services, capabilities).

Environmental forces are not static. As is true with all marketing, the only constant is change. This point is important: Marketing is an exchange process that is not fixed or passive but is active, cyclical, and ever-changing.

Change can work for you or against you. Creative marketing is finding ways to make change work for you.

Technological forces: developments in telecommunications, computers, transportation modes, construction, automation, bioengineering, genetics, medicine, and educational delivery systems (laser disc information storage and retrieval), which have a profound influence on our society and on nonprofit organizations.

Technological forces can offer threats as well as opportunities to an organization. For example, once almost every engineer owned a slide rule. Sales of slide rules were critical to the primary supplier, Keuffel & Esser. The advent of computers and hand-held calculators quickly made the slide rule obsolete, but K&E did not anticipate this technological shift. Although K&E had the necessary resources to develop computers and calculators, it did not move into this new market. Thus, K&E lost its niche in the marketplace.

Political forces: local, state, and federal legislation; regulation; agency policies; program priorities; and funding. Developments in government relations with the nonprofit sector have an enormous effect on most nonprofit organizations. You need to keep up-to-date on how your organization relates to the ever-changing political scene.

For most nonprofits, political leaders and administrators are a key component of their target audiences, and, in some cases, legislators and politicians may form an important target audience themselves, one requiring careful attention. For example, the effects of federal legislation to limit financial aid to students were serious for many colleges and universities whose students were forced by economic constraints to limit their studies to part time or to drop out altogether. Often nonprofits fail to consider the political implications when they are developing and delivering programs to target groups. As with the other forces, political forces can work with you or against you, and the way you market your organization can be critical in determining how the forces affect you.

Another example of the effect of political forces involves a program by the federal government to limit Medicare and Medicaid costs for health care. The government's adoption of DRGs (Diagnostic Related Groups) has had a great impact on nonprofit health care organizations. The government set prices for reimbursement for procedures in connection with 467 diseases. As you can imagine, the impact on hospitals and health care organizations has been dramatic. Some have found ways to take advantage of the DRG "imposition" by carefully controlling costs through computer accounting systems and utilization review committees. But others have not and are struggling with costs that exceed federal reimbursements; this has a serious effect on the bottom line.

Competitive forces: efforts by competing organizations to control, acquire, and expand their market share (groups of current or potential consumers). For nonprofits, competition can come from profit-motivated companies as well as other nonprofits. For example, the proliferation of freestanding, profit-making, 24-hour-a-day medical clinics provides competition for hospital emergency rooms.

Examine the current and potential competitive forces that may affect your organization (see Chapter 7). Now is the time to plan ways to control current competition and to anticipate future competition.

Economic forces: trends such as economic growth, recession, consumer spending behavior, real estate values, employment/unemployment, inflation, interest rates, rates of business investment, stock prices, business development, credit availability, and corporate philanthropy. Some of the strongest forces in our society today are economic ones.

Think about the influence of inflation on most nonprofits in the late 1970s and early 1980s. For many it has severely changed the way they operate.

Each of these economic forces has implications that affect, directly or indirectly, both sides of your marketing planning map. The economic forces that affect your organization also affect your external audiences. In most cases these influences are profound. You need to study them carefully and anticipate their effects if you possibly can.

Societal forces: factors such as population growth, geographical distribution, family composition, birth rate, age, sex, education, income, occupation, social class, business trends, and changes in lifestyles. Changes in these forces may influence health (many people are improving their health through "trendy" exercise such as aerobics or jogging), leisure (a shorter work week means more time for leisure activities), and nutrition (more processed and frozen foods are on the market for families that have less time to cook).

The effects of these forces can be quantitative (such as changes in demographics) or qualitative (such as changes in lifestyles).

The way your organization organizes its skills and resources should relate to the environment in which it operates. For example, a community college located in an area of high unemployment would not need to offer courses in tax shelters but might consider courses in new employment technologies.

What you do, how you do it, when you do it, and where you do it should be based, to a great degree, on strategies that grow out of your understanding of these external forces. Use Worksheet 19 at the end of this chapter to describe how external forces affect your organization.

Exploring the universe

Let's look again at the marketing planning map. The external forces impact on the universe as well as on your organization. Every nonprofit has a universe that consists of its target markets. A target market is a group of people that matter to your organization—now or in the future. They may be customers or other key groups such as political groups, funding sources, or prospective customers. They rank high on your list as a result of evaluative criteria you have established. Each target market group represents a segment of your total market universe. Collectively these target markets are vital to the mission of your organization.

Market segmentation can help you understand your marketing universe. Market segmentation is a way of breaking down the total universe into cohesive, discrete groups. This is done by screening the universe according to criteria you have established. These criteria may be geographic, economic, demographic, types of lifestyle, needs, or any of the forces just discussed. (See Worksheet 8, page 58, for a list of segmentation variables.)

Once you have established your target markets, you must understand them. Understanding your target markets can help you develop better services, better delivery, better communication, and better promotion—all of which lead to better marketing. Target marketing is also more economical; no organization can afford to market all of its services to all of the people all of the time. If you have a clear idea about the target market you are aiming for, it will help you every step of the marketing way.

On the marketing planning map, note that your universe is depicted as a circle with your target markets inside. I call this the "circle of opportunity." As I've stressed throughout this guidebook, a nonprofit organization needs to market itself from the outside in, not from the inside out. Understanding your external audiences—your target markets—offers you this circle of opportunity, your chance to apply marketing skills to advance your organization.

Describe your target markets by answering the following questions:

- Who are your target markets?
- Where are they?
- How many people are included in each target market?
- What are their common characteristics?
- Why are they important?
- What are their needs and wants? How can your organization best serve them?
- How can you identify new target markets?
- What products could you develop to better serve current markets?
- What products would attract new target markets?
- How does one target market overlap another? What advantage is this to you?

Target markets provide your organization with its reason to exist. A college or university cannot exist without students, faculty, and alumni. A health care organization cannot exist without patients, doctors, nurses, and support staff. A symphony cannot exist without patrons, a zoo without visitors, a city government without citizens, a politician without voters.

When you segment a universe into target markets, you must first think about all the ways people differ. They think differently; behave differently; live in different places; earn different incomes; have different jobs, hobbies, skills, and interests. In fact, every human being is different from every other human being. Thus, to identify a target market, you must identify certain characteristics that are shared by groups of people.

You then break down your market by these characteristics, or segmenting criteria. For example, if you work for a YMCA that offers fitness services, you will probably segment by location, marketing to people who live within a five-mile radius of the "Y." If you're marketing for a symphony orchestra, you may want to market to people identified by income range or to people who are interested in the arts or to people who live in a certain area known for its cultured lifestyle. Or you might want to segment by educational level, marketing young people's concerts to grammar school students, for example.

You can segment markets by behavioral characteristics. Each market segment behaves differently. Some people will be receptive to your products; others will resist them. Ask yourself why. Find the answer by studying each target market's attitudes, values, personalities, lifestyle, social class, family role, and cultural group.

Target marketing is simple. You want to match, to the greatest possible extent, people who are most likely to be interested in your services. Market segmentation helps you make the match efficiently and effectively between potential users and your organization's services.

Refer back to Worksheet 4 in Chapter 5 (page 31). If you have not already filled out this worksheet, use it now to segment your universe into target markets. Try to identify a market segment for each service your organization offers. You will identify many target audiences. Some of these audiences may overlap as indicated on the marketing planning map. Take advantage of this overlap if you can. For example, you may be able to piggyback one marketing effort on another to reach a common target market. You need to consider other ways overlap can work to help your marketing ventures. Evaluate each target market by itself and in relationship to other target markets.

Think about the size of each target market—how many people are included—and, if relevant, how much time and/or money they can spend. For example, if you work for an educational organization with a membership that is 42 percent fund raisers and 2 percent government relations professionals, you would be foolish to spend equal amounts of staff time and budget on each of these segments. You also have to consider how each target market relates to your organization's mission. You will want to pay particular attention to those markets that rate high on a composite of evaluative criteria. Simply put, expend valuable resources and efforts in areas that have the greatest potential payoff.

Accessibility should also affect your marketing efforts. Some of your target markets may be directly accessible; you can contact them through various forms of direct communication. Others may be indirectly accessible. They are influenced by others through word-of-mouth referral—a patient is referred to a health care facility by his doctor; a student applies to a college because her mother went there.

Competition is also an important factor. You need to know who your competitors are, how much effort they are expending to reach your target markets, and how that effort compares to yours.

Product mix and target market mix

Your organization probably offers a mix of services that varies over time. There will also be a mix of target audiences for these services. How you control your product mix in relation to your target market mix over time is important. You may offer a once-popular service to an important target market and, over the years, see that market dissipate because you have not adapted the service to the changing market. The skillful marketer should find ways to keep that market alive when the particular service no longer appeals. A marketing time-line can help by showing services in relationship to target market considerations.

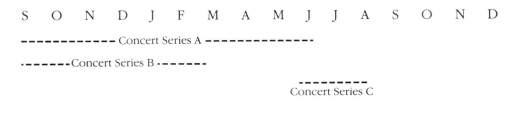

Figure 14: Marketing Time-line Monthly Calendar

Figure 14 is a marketing time-line for a symphony orchestra that offers three concert series during the year: a series of light classics for high school students, per-
formed throughout the academic year (Concert Series A); a fall/winter concert series
targeted at adult patrons interested in traditional music (Concert Series B); and an
outdoor summertime pops concert series targeted at business professionals (Concert Series C). As the time-line shows, the three concert series overlap in time. Target
audiences may also overlap. The high school students might enjoy the pops concerts; some of the business professionals may attend the Series B concerts, and
so on. Mailings for Series C may be piggybacked onto Series A and Series B mailings. Inserts in Series A and B concert programs could promote Series C.

The marketing time-line calendar is important to timing. You can bet that profit-
motivated corporations do not drop products into the marketplace whenever they
feel like it. They plot and strategize their product entries carefully. They know that
product and target market relationships and timing are critical to eventual success.
Plan your services mix and marketing time-line calendar carefully.

You may want to post a marketing time-line calendar in your office. Identify each
of your services and related target markets on it. Plot each service over time. Worksheet 5 (page 32) may be helpful. Study relationships. What opportunities do you
see? What problems? You may want to include competitive services. How do these
affect your services?

By now I hope you are beginning to get a feel for nonprofit marketing. It's a lot
like conducting a symphony orchestra. You have many resources, just as a con-
ductor has resources (woodwinds, strings, brass, percussion), and it's your job to
"orchestrate" these resources. Your marketing plan is the musical score that tells
you how to conduct your marketing orchestra. You can make loud sounds or quiet
ones. Some can last a long time; others can be short. You can mix resources based
on what you want to do. How well your audience responds to your performance
depends on how well you create and execute your marketing plan.

Using research to support your marketing plan

Again, look at the marketing planning map on page 126. Note that the box below
the circle of opportunity is labeled "Marketing information." Many profit-motivated
corporations maintain well-staffed marketing research departments or buy research
services to acquire marketing information. Marketing information is just as impor-

tant for your nonprofit organization.

Lots of marketing research information is available. Some creative sleuthing on your part will reveal sources of important marketing information. Look for information that can be used to project trends and that can help you better understand your universe, your services, and your organization. You may be surprised at how much information you find. You need information that bridges the gap between your target markets and your organization's services. You should also collect information that explores new target markets, helps you improve or find new services, or predicts trends that will affect your services and your marketing efforts in the future. Be creative! Don't limit your thinking. Consider information that will help you examine the broad issues as well as facts that will help you with the details.

Start by auditing each segment of your organization to find out what research data exist. A good place to start is with the U.S. Census. You can gain lots of valuable information about population trends, including population shifts that may have direct impact on your nonprofit's services.

Local mailing services may be able to provide helpful marketing data. Your local mailing service company has access to commercially prepared lists organized by subject areas (people who subscribe to specific magazines or belong to certain clubs, for example). Lists organized by geographics (ZIP codes and carrier routes) and by combined factors of lifestyle, income level, residence, and occupation may help you in marketing planning and execution.

Your local library probably has excellent files. Chambers of commerce maintain data about trends, developments, demographics, and growth. Newspapers (because of their interest in advertising sales) are good sources of information about your community and its target markets. Service organizations, such as local and state agencies, are good sources for valuable marketing research information.

In the field of health care, for instance, federal, state, and local organizations gather data about hospitals. Data about treatment by medical specialty, length of stay, number of inpatients and outpatients, and cost reimbursements can provide valuable information to a competitive marketer. If a professional organization represents your nonprofit service sector, it should be a good source of research information.

The process of gathering, reviewing, and exploring market research information is often best done by teams of people. It can be exciting and rewarding work. A team of your colleagues, along with representatives of your target markets, staff, administrators, volunteers, board of directors, and others will be able to serve as a marketing research information task force.

Consider developing a team for each of your services and another to gather information for your generic organization as well. In this way, you will have information about specific product lines and about the parent organization. This information will be very useful when you prepare your marketing plans. In Chapters 9 and 11 we discussed the "umbrella" concept shown in Figure 15; the umbrella is the parent nonprofit organization with the various product lines (services) appearing under the umbrella in clusters that reflect organizational structure.

The umbrella organizational model is common in commercial, profit-motivated organizations. General Motors, for example, is the generic parent umbrella organi-

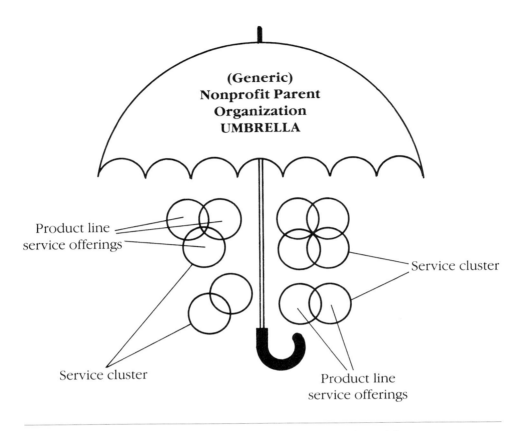

Figure 15: Nonprofit Organizational Model

zation for Chevrolet, Pontiac, and Cadillac. Each service cluster offers specific product lines (cars, trucks). Each product is identified by its name (Cadillac Eldorado). Think of your organization in similar ways. This marketing organizational model will provide a convenient framework for marketing your nonprofit organization and its services.

Don't be put off by this comparison to General Motors. I am not suggesting that your organization adopt profit-motivated processes. I am, however, suggesting that you can learn a great deal from studying how corporate groups organize, market, and promote themselves.

So far we've focused on the left side of the marketing planning map—the external factors—because I strongly advocate marketing nonprofit services from the outside in, not from the inside out. To be a successful marketer you must understand the marketing world around you.

Now it's time to look at the right side of the map, which describes your organization. You must analyze your nonprofit organization before you can market it effectively to target audiences. You may be tempted to say, "I know my organization, its mission, and services. This will be easy." A word of caution: One of the most difficult aspects of marketing a nonprofit organization is understanding it *as it is perceived from external points of view.* Remember the adage, "You can't see the forest for the trees." Many people have such a strong commitment to the nonprofit they work for that it's almost impossible for them to be objective about it. They are simply too dedicated to their nonprofit to view it as others experience it or perceive it. This can be a fatal flaw.

One way to get around this problem is to create a marketing/development/ advancement steering committee. This committee should include internal and external representatives, and these individuals should be people who are respected for their unbiased, clear thinking.

If your nonprofit is small, this committee will be able to execute its duties easily. But if your nonprofit organization is large, the steering committee may need to function as an administrative group for other marketing teams (organized by services to cut across traditional organizational boundaries).

These subcommittees will be action groups that explore the marketing planning map. They should examine your organization as it relates to your marketing planning map. Encourage them to use the map to help plan marketing for their service lines. They will prepare and manage the action plans, and the steering committee will monitor their efforts.

Remember that effective marketing cannot be a solo effort; it must be a team effort with many people working together to achieve common marketing goals and objectives.

Your steering committee starts with the Four P's of marketing:

• **P**roduct: a service provided to satisfy the desires and needs of a target audience;

• **P**rice: costs related to the marketing exchange between service provider and users; in some cases, costs may be intangible (time and effort) as well as monetary;

• **P**lace: the location where a nonprofit service is provided to a user; and

• **P**romotion: advertising and other forms of activities (public relations, sales, publicity) used to encourage the marketing exchange process.

Use Worksheet 20, "The Four P's of Marketing," to make an inventory of your services. List the Four P's for each service. Be sure to consider every aspect of each offering. This inventory will provide a marketing picture of your nonprofit's current offerings and serve as a starting point when you are exploring new offerings and opportunities.

Your steering committee can use the inventory of the Four P's to build a research base that will include two categories: internal and external research. Internal research (such as the Four P's) focuses on your services as seen from your organization's point of view. External research focuses on your services as perceived by external constituents (target markets).

Use this research to build four plans (in the order given):

• *The program plan.* The program plan outlines services your nonprofit organization offers. It describes current and future services, target markets, and plans for the development and advancement of services as influenced by external forces. Although the program plan considers external marketing aspects, it is primarily an internally focused plan. Most nonprofits have traditionally developed a program plan so it is not a new idea.

• *The business plan.* The business plan, the financial part of your marketing study, outlines income and expenses. It should consider all aspects covered by a traditional financial plan (personnel costs, materials, overhead, and other expenses). Most nonprofits routinely prepare an annual fiscal-year plan. Incremental (department) budgets are components of a traditional business plan. You may want to consider creating a financial plan that covers a longer period of time (two or three years) in order to relate more closely to your long-range marketing plan.

The business plan will not be a new idea for your organization. It has probably been using one for many years to control expenses and income.

• *The marketing plan.* The marketing plan may be a new idea. It links the program and business plans with the outside world. Unlike the program and business plans, it has an external focus. The marketing plan relates internal services to external audiences (target markets).

For a nonprofit organization, the relationship between program plan, business plan, and marketing plan is critical. Many nonprofits that have accepted and implemented marketing find that the marketing plan becomes very valuable. Because marketing is closer to the consumer, marketing efforts reveal valuable information that can be used to influence current and future program and business plans.

For many nonprofits, the marketing plan will suggest actions while the organization's program and business plans are traditionally passive documents.

• *The promotional plan.* This plan develops directly from the marketing plan. To be effective, a promotional plan must emerge from information gathered by and presented in the marketing plan. Developing a promotional plan without a marketing plan is folly; the result will be based on guesswork, hunches, and seat-of-the-pants speculation.

Thus, marketing forces synergy between an organization's program, business, marketing, and promotional plans.

Look again at the marketing planning map. The last box under "Your nonprofit organization" is "Evaluation of results." Evaluation is what you do to gather information that is useful in marketing. You measure programs and services by evaluation. This evaluation must be both internal (from the organization's viewpoint) and external (from target markets' and constituents' viewpoints).

The three boxes in the right-hand column of the marketing planning map should provide a basis for action plans. You begin to develop action plans by examining your organization's mission. If your organization does not have a viable mission statement, you must create one (see Chapter 4). The mission statement provides the foundation for your marketing planning and activities.

This mission statement should include your organization's major goals, its philosophy, its current commitments, and its vision for the future. Growing out of your mission statement is a description of your services to various target markets as well as desired fiscal and quantitative outcomes, especially over the long term (three to five years).

Next, you must study your nonprofit's objectives. List quantitative goals based on organizational mission. What needs to be accomplished by a certain time? These goals must be specific and measurable. They will serve as benchmarks of performance. They will provide valuable research information.

Next is positioning—how your organization's services are perceived by external target markets as compared to competitive services. You must determine how target markets perceive each of your organization's products and services as compared to competitive products and services.

On Worksheet 21 at the end of this chapter, write a statement for each of your services, describing its key aspects or features. Use research from target markets to describe these key elements. You should be able to identify which of your services your competitors cannot deliver as well as your organization can, according to external target audiences. For these services your organization has a comparative differential advantage.

Organizing, budgeting, and scheduling make up the next step. These are the "mechanical" parts of your action plans. Don't overlook their importance. Review them carefully in relation to your other action plans. They make the marketing plan work. They enable you to translate marketing concepts into actions.

You have now completed your journey through the marketing planning map. The trip may have seemed long and complicated, but I hope that you have become familiar with the landmarks—the components of the marketing process. Each landmark leads you further on your way to your destination. Each of these marketing components can be studied, planned, and executed. And when you have done this, you will be able to enjoy a successful marketing trip.

For further reading

Kotler, Philip. *Marketing for Nonprofit Organizations.* Englewood Cliffs, NJ: Prentice-Hall, 1975; revised 1982.

Kotler, Philip, and Fox, Karen F.A. *Strategic Marketing for Educational Institutions.* Englewood Cliffs, NJ: Prentice-Hall, 1985.

Topor, Robert S. *Marketing Cooperative Extension.* Ithaca, NY: Cornell University Media Services, 1982.

Topor, Robert S. *Marketing Cooperative Extension—The Organization.* Videotape. Washington, DC: United States Department of Agriculture, 1986.

Topor, Robert S. *Marketing Higher Education: A Practical Guide.* Washington, DC: Council for Advancement and Support of Education, 1983.

Is your nonprofit organization truly consumer- (market-) driven? Measure your organization's current status in terms of marketing and consumer orientation. Is your organization really oriented towards important outside audiences? How well does your organization explore the marketing planning map (see page 126)? How well does it apply marketing principles—not only in theory but in reality? How well is your organization prepared to deliver a marketing-driven service? How well does your organization implement its marketing activities?

Marketing Self-test

1. Your nonprofit organization's orientation to personal service is created by:

☐ Yes ☐ No Having a director, coordinator, or project manager primarily responsible to the user.

☐ Yes ☐ No A series of motivational workshops for all staff and employees.

☐ Yes ☐ No Telephone courtesies and first-impression training.

☐ Yes ☐ No Special parking privileges for "customers" or users.

☐ Yes ☐ No Inclusion of courtesy standards on performance appraisal forms.

☐ Yes ☐ No Advertising that is created from research to determine the best features your organization offers.

☐ Yes ☐ No A clearly defined mission statement that everyone can understand and to which all services can be related.

☐ Yes ☐ No Public relations efforts clearly directed toward target market groups.

☐ Yes ☐ No A promotional plan that supports and works with your marketing plan.

☐ Yes ☐ No Clearly understanding needs and wants of target markets.

2. Many of your administrators, managers, or service providers believe that:

☐ Yes ☐ No They have to do a lot of convincing to get others to participate in marketing activities.

☐ Yes ☐ No Salary and written performance standards are the same for good workers as they are for those who are mediocre.

☐ Yes ☐ No They don't need to do market research to determine target markets' needs and wants; they can rely on "gut" feelings.

☐ Yes ☐ No The "customer" is not always right; your organization knows what is best for the user.

3. Many of your staff and employees believe that:

☐ Yes ☐ No   Their well-being is not a top priority of their supervisor.

☐ Yes ☐ No   They don't have time to "be nice."

☐ Yes ☐ No   Efforts to become more personal-oriented are primarily directed at their colleagues rather than at users.

☐ Yes ☐ No   Marketing will go away.

4. Management systems are in place to:

☐ Yes ☐ No   Remove long-term rude, disgruntled employees.

☐ Yes ☐ No   Remove deadwood.

☐ Yes ☐ No   Expand nontraditional hiring and selection to screen for personal as well as technical expertise.

☐ Yes ☐ No   Rapidly discipline and, if necessary, dismiss employees who are not contributing to the marketing parts of their job descriptions.

☐ Yes ☐ No   Provide appropriate training to help employees understand and implement marketing activities.

☐ Yes ☐ No   Reward outstanding service through appropriate monetary and recognition rewards.

5. The following measures are tied to performance appraisal, pay increases, promotions, and employee recognition:

☐ Yes ☐ No   Internal data systems exist to pinpoint those departments or units that meet or exceed standards for "customer" satisfaction and good employee/staff relations.

☐ Yes ☐ No   Frequent reviews of operating procedures to measure marketing effectiveness are in place.

Your organization's effort to become more market-driven may be seriously flawed if you answered "no" to a majority of the statements in items 1, 4, and 5, and you answered "yes" to a majority of the statements in items 2 and 3.

Worksheet 19

External Forces

EXTERNAL FORCES   INFLUENCE ON YOUR:

	Target market	Competition	Organization's services
1. Environmental forces			
2. Technological forces			
3. Political forces			
4. Competitive forces			
5. Economic forces			
6. Societal forces			

List the ways that each external force influences your target market, your competitors, and your organization's services. For each force, list current developments, movements, changes, factors, and processes that influence or have impact on your organization, its programs, and its activities.

When completed, this worksheet will provide a valuable matrix of information. It will paint a picture of the effect of all the different forces on your organization as well as on your target markets. You will be able to see how external forces influence your competition. This will help you position your services and your organization. Positioning is the way external audiences perceive your services and your organization as compared to competitors. Understanding positioning will help you find ways to project a competitive differential advantage to your target markets.

Worksheet 20

The Four P's of Marketing

Product (service)

Price

Place (location)

Promotion

Product. Fill out a copy of this worksheet for each of your organization's services. Describe the service under the heading "Product (services)." Be sure to list all aspects of each service. Consider external as well as internal perceptions. Describe the service in terms of how it fills the user's needs and satisfies his or her wants. Keep your descriptions simple. Describe the service's core concept. What is it intended to do? Describe its attributes. Keep in mind how the service relates to competitive services in the marketplace.

Price. List all real costs (from the user's point of view). Costs may be real or hidden, tangible or intangible. For example, a concert-goer may spend money to buy a ticket and time to attend a performance. A "customer" may expend time to attend a free educational lecture.

Place. Location of services, in marketing as in real estate, is critical. The user's convenience is vital to marketing your product. List all locations of your service.

Promotion. Describe ways that this service is promoted or can be promoted. Collect promotional samples for each service. Consider each form of media (see Chapter 12, Selecting Promotional Media: A Guide).

141

Worksheet 21

Your Organization's Services

Service	Target market	Critical match

In the first column, list services your organization provides. Remember that marketing is an exchange process. List anything that you offer for which an external user will exchange his or her resources. These services may be tangible items (books) or intangible items (knowledge).

Think of your services in terms of users. How can you describe each user group (demographics, lifestyle, geographics, psychographics)?

In the third column, list reasons for the target market to have real or potential interest in your services. At first, you may feel that this worksheet has little or no value to you, that you already understand your organization's services, as well as your "customers" and their reasons for using your services. But once this worksheet is completed, especially if it is prepared by a group of people, you may be surprised at the results.

The process of filling out this worksheet will help you unify staff, explore current and new services, and better understand your target markets.

If yours is a large nonprofit organization, prepare a worksheet for each service. Compile the sheets by organizational structure (units, departments). You might want to prepare a worksheet for each department and one for the total organization as well.

The completed document will provide you with an excellent resource for planning marketing strategies. It will also provide a historical benchmark for evaluation.

Chapter 16

Your Nonprofit Marketing Compass

Marketing a nonprofit organization is a lot like traveling in a new territory. It helps to have a map and a compass to chart your course and find your way. There are many directions you could go. There are many different routes to your goal, some more direct than others.

The secret of success is to pick your path carefully and to focus attention on the paths that are most critical at this time. Remember that long journeys comprise many small steps. You need to consider long-term and short-term goals. Set your long-term goals at the high level you would like to reach some day, but be conservative when you set short-term goals.

The nonprofit marketing compass (Figure 16) can help you identify your long-term goals in several service marketing areas. It can also help you identify the focus for successful short-term efforts.

Notice that the compass has 10 spokes. The spokes represent 10 important marketing focal points that you need to consider in marketing your organization and its services. You can use the compass to measure where you are today in your marketing efforts and to set your sights on where you want to be at some time in the future. That time may be next month, next year, or two years from now. It's up to you to pick the time frame.

Notice that the spokes of the marketing compass are arranged in logical order:
1. external forces analysis;
2. mission;
3. research;
4. product;
5. place;
6. price;
7. promotion;
8. target markets;

143

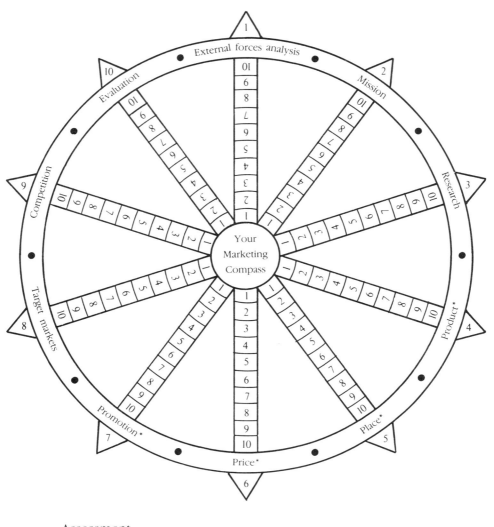

Assessment: _____

* The four P's of marketing

Summary

Make photocopies of this compass for each service you are going to assess. Make one that represents your entire nonprofit organization.

Step 1: Where are you now? (Draw a line across the arrow at the appropriate number.)

Step 2: Where do you want to be in the long term? (Draw a dotted line at the appropriate number.)

Step 3: For each area (spoke) draw a third line one number greater than your current level. Shade in the space between that line and your step 1 line (current level) to show your short-term goal for improvement.

Figure 16: Your Nonprofit Marketing Compass:
Charting Your Course Through the Marketing Planning Map

144

9. competition; and

10. evaluation.

Note that these elements relate to the marketing planning map on page 126. They are the key marketing "directions" that are important to achieve successful marketing. But unlike a traditional compass, when you use this one, it doesn't lead you in only one direction. To advance in marketing, you must be proceeding in almost *all* directions at the same time. You need to advance on many fronts.

How to use your nonprofit marketing compass

You can use the compass to assess current status and to identify potential improvement for a specific service, or you can use it to assess current status and goals for your entire organization. For best results, you should prepare a compass for each service your organization markets. You should also produce a master compass that represents the whole organization.

Step 1: Determine what it is you are going to assess, a specific service or the whole organization. Let's say you are going to assess a particular service. Write the name of the service on the line labeled "Assessment" on Figure 16. Begin at point 1 on the compass, "External Forces Analysis." A score of "10" on this spoke means peak performance on this element for the service you are rating. A score of "1" is the lowest point on the scale and indicates no activity in this area. You may want to consider input from others to help you determine the rating. Get opinions from people on your marketing committee. Tabulate results. Then draw a line at that number across the spoke.

Go through the same process for all the other marketing spokes on the wheel.

Step 2. Go back to each spoke of the compass and draw a dotted line across the spoke at the number you hope to reach some day. The difference between the two lines on each spoke is your opportunity for desired improvement, your gap of opportunity. (See Figure 17 for an example of a completed marketing compass.)

Step 3. Now go back to the compass and draw a third line only one number higher than your current level (the line you draw for step 1) and shade in the area between the two lines as in Figure 17.

Summary

Your goal for the time frame you have identified is to accomplish improvement in the shaded areas. That small, achievable improvement will be the basis for building a successful marketing plan. Set your short-term objectives around those identified small goals and plan to achieve success. When those plans are accomplished, use the compass to select the next stage of improvement on your way to successful marketing.

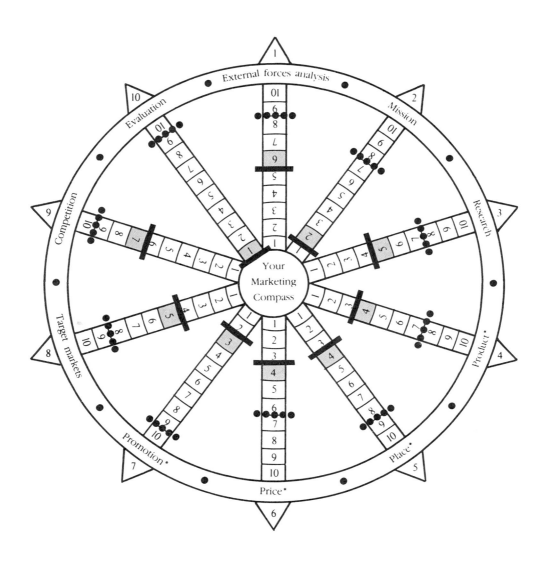

Figure 17: Your Completed Nonprofit Marketing Compass

Summary

Congratulations! You have completed your study of *Your Personal Guide to Marketing a Nonprofit Organization.* I hope it's been both enjoyable and rewarding. Now you are ready to be a guide to others in your organization. You have learned the answer to the question, "What is marketing for a nonprofit organization?" You've learned to lay the groundwork for your marketing efforts in several ways:

- by understanding your organization's political environment;
- by defining your organization's mission;
- by segmenting your markets; and
- by using research to analyze your competition and your target markets and their needs.

You've learned the techniques of promotion, advertising, and sales—methods by which you reach out to your target markets. You've made your way through the marketing planning map. You've used hte marketing compass to assess your services. If you've done the worksheets, you've already outlined the essentials of your own marketing plan. You are now ready to begin your marketing efforts in earnest.

Working for a nonprofit organization can be very rewarding. Nonprofit services are important to us; they represent people helping people put knowledge to work. Your place in this world is very special. Use marketing to help your organization succeed. Use marketing to preserve your organization and help it flourish.

Bibliography

Basic marketing texts

Kotler, Philip. *Marketing for Nonprofit Organizations*. Englewood Cliffs, NJ: Prentice-Hall, 1975; revised 1982. Written by a professor at Northwestern University, this is one of the best books describing marketing and image-building techniques for nonprofit organizations. In an easy-to-read style, Kotler describes marketing techniques and ways to apply them to higher education and other nonprofit organizations.

Kotler, Philip, and Andreasen, Alan R. *Strategic Marketing for Nonprofit Organizations,* 3rd ed. Englewood Cliffs, NJ: Prentice-Hall, 1987. This revision of *Marketing for Nonprofit Organizations* is an excellent resource tool for the person who is familiar with basic marketing concepts and wishes to apply advanced nonprofit strategic marketing concepts. The book is organized into four parts: developing a customer orientation, strategic planning and organization, designing the marketing mix, and controlling marketing strategies. It includes case studies from a variety of nonprofits—museums, universities, libraries, hospitals, and theaters. "Must" reading for the advanced practitioner.

Kotler, Philip, and Fox, Karen F. A. *Strategic Marketing for Educational Institutions*. Englewood Cliffs, NJ: Prentice-Hall, 1985. This book examines marketing concepts and tools for administrators in colleges, universities, and private schools. The book's strategic planning perspective, numerous examples, and careful organization help advancement professionals apply marketing and image-building concepts to their institutions.

Topor, Robert S. *Institutional Image: How to Define, Improve, Market It*. Washington, DC: Council for Advancement and Support of Education, 1986. Written primarily for institutions of higher education, this book can be used by any nonprofit organization. It describes how an organization can use market research to determine its image in the marketplace. It tells who should be involved in building an institution's image, how to position the institution in the competitive marketplace, and how to better communicate an institution's strengths and qualities to improve its image.

Topor, Robert S. *Marketing Higher Education: A Practical Guide*. Washington, DC: Council for Advancement and Support of Education, 1983. Designed for the newcomer to institutional marketing, this guide describes how to apply marketing concepts and techniques. It helps advancement professionals analyze target audience needs; improve products, services, and communications; and become more effective administrators. Subjects covered include marketing strategies, research, services, events, communications, image perception, audience segmentation, and positioning.

Other nonprofit marketing references

Adler, Mortimer T. *How to Speak/How to Listen.* New York: Macmillan, 1983.

Bagozzi, Richard. *Marketing in the 80's: Changes and Challenges.* Chicago: American Marketing Association, 1980.

Barton-Gillet Company. "The Communications Process in Marketing." Baltimore, MD: 1969.

Bennett, Claude. *Reflective Appraisal of Programs.* Ithaca, NY: Cornell University Media Services, 1982.

Berlo, David K. *The Process of Communication.* New York: Holt, Rinehart and Winston, 1960.

Blankenship, A.B. *Professional Telephone Surveys.* New York: McGraw-Hill, 1977.

Bogart, Leo. *Strategy in Advertising.* New York: Harcourt, Brace and World, 1967.

Book, Albert C., and Schick, C. Dennis. *Fundamentals of Copy and Layout.* Lincolnwood, IL: National Textbook Co. Business Books, 1986.

Boone, Louis E., and Kurtz, David L. *Contemporary Marketing.* Hinsdale, IL: Dryden Press, 1977.

Brandt, Steven C. *Entrepreneuring—The 10 Commandments for Building a Growth Company.* New York: New American Library, 1982.

Cetron, Marvin, and O'Toole, Thomas. *Encounters with the Future: A Forecast of Life into the 21st Century.* New York: McGraw-Hill, 1972.

Cochran, William C. *Sampling Techniques,* 2nd ed. New York: John Wiley & Sons, 1963.

Council for Advancement and Support of Education. "What Is Market Research? What Can It Do for Me?" CASE CURRENTS, May/June 1982.

Crane, Edgar. *Marketing Communications.* New York: John Wiley & Sons, 1972.

Dillman, Don A. *Mail and Telephone Surveys: The Total Design Method.* New York: John Wiley & Sons, 1978.

Drucker, Peter F. *Managing for Results.* New York: Harper & Row, 1964.

Erdos, Paul. *Professional Mail Surveys.* New York: McGraw-Hill, 1970.

Ferber, Robert, ed. *Handbook of Marketing Research.* New York: McGraw-Hill, 1974.

Fine, Seymour H. *The Marketing of Ideas and Social Issues.* New York: Praeger Publishers, 1981.

Flint, Emily P., ed. *Creative Editing and Writing Workbook.* Washington, DC: Council for Advancement and Support of Education, 1979.

Fowler, Charles R. "Making Marketing Work: How a coordinated approach improved a college's enrollment, retention, and public image." CURRENTS, November/December 1983, pp. 20-22.

Francis, J. Bruce, ed. *Surveying Institutional Constituencies.* San Francisco: Jossey-Bass, 1979.

Goldman, Jordan. *Public Relations in the Marketing Mix—Introducing Vulnerability Relations.* Chicago: Crain Books, 1984.

Goldstein, Sherry, and Kravetz, Ellen, eds. *Findex: The Directory of Market Research Reports, Studies and Surveys,* 5th ed. New York: Find/SVP, 1983.

Group Attitudes Corporation. *American Attitudes Toward Higher Education,* 2 vols. New York: Hill & Knowlton, 1982, 1983, 1984.

Hamilton, Seymour. *A Communication Audit Handbook—Helping Organizations Communicate.* New York: Longman, 1987.

Ihlanfeldt, William. "A Management Approach to the Buyer's Market." *Liberal Education,* May 1975, pp. 133-148.

Keller, George. *Academic Strategy: The Management Revolution in American Education.* Baltimore, MD: Johns Hopkins University Press, 1983.

Kotler, Philip. *Marketing Management: Analysis, Planning and Control,* 3rd ed. Englewood Cliffs, NJ: Prentice-Hall, 1976.

Kotler, Philip, et al. *Cases and Readings for Marketing for Nonprofit Organizations.* Englewood Cliffs, NJ: Prentice-Hall, 1983.

Kress, George. *Marketing Research,* 2nd ed. Reston, VA: Reston Publishing Co., 1982.

Levitt, Theodore. *The Marketing Imagination.* New York: Free Press, 1983.

Levitt, Theodore. "Marketing Myopia." *Harvard Business Review,* July/August 1960, pp. 45-56.

Lindenmann, Walter K. *Attitude and Opinion Research: Why You Need It/How to Do It,* 3rd ed. Washington, DC: Council for Advancement and Support of Education, 1983.

Lovelock, Christopher H., and Weinberg, Charles B. *Marketing for Public and Nonprofit Managers.* New York: John Wiley & Sons, 1984.

McCormack, Mark H. *What They Don't Teach You at Harvard Business School.* New York: Bantam Books, 1984.

McGown, K.L. *Marketing Research—Text and Cases.* Cambridge, MA: Winthrop Publishers, 1979.

McMillan, Norman H. *Marketing Your Hospital: A Strategy for Survival.* Chicago: American Hospital Association, 1981.

Moll, Richard W. "A Flower Child Grows Up: Responding to changing times at UC Santa Cruz." CURRENTS, November/December 1983, pp. 16-18.

Naisbitt, John. *Megatrends.* New York: Warner Books, 1984.

Nie, Norman, et al. *SPSS,* 2nd ed. New York: McGraw-Hill, 1975.

Ogilvy, David. *Ogilvy on Advertising.* New York: Vintage Books, Random House, 1985.

Ohmae, Kenichi. *The Mind of the Strategist—Business Planning for Competitive Advantage.* New York: Penguin Books, 1986.

Opinion Research Corporation. *American Attitudes Toward Higher Education.* New York: 1985.

Payne, Stanley. *The Art of Asking Questions: Studies in Public Opinion.* Princeton, NJ: Princeton University Press, 1954, 1980.

Peters, Tom. *Thriving on Chaos—Handbook for a Management Revolution.* New York: Alfred A. Knopf, 1987.

Peters, Tom, and Austin, Nancy. *A Passion for Excellence.* New York: Random House, 1985.

Peters, Tom, and Waterman, Robert H., Jr. *In Search of Excellence.* New York: Warner Books, 1982.

Public Interest Public Relations, Inc. *Promoting Issues & Ideas, A Guide to Public Relations for Nonprofit Organizations.* New York: The Foundation Center, 1987.

Ray, Michael, and Myers, Rochelle. *Creativity in Business.* Garden City, NJ: Double-day, 1986.

Ries, Al, and Trout, Jack. *Marketing Warfare.* New York: McGraw-Hill, 1986.

Ries, Al, and Trout, Jack. *Positioning: The Battle for Your Mind.* New York: McGraw-Hill, 1981.

Rogers, Everett M., and Shoemaker, F. Floyd. *Communication of Innovations.* New York: Free Press, 1971.

Roman, Kenneth, and Maas, Jane. *How to Advertise.* New York: St. Martin's Press, 1977.

Rowland, A. Westley, gen. ed. *Handbook of Institutional Advancement,* 2nd ed. San Francisco: Jossey-Bass, 1986.

Selame, Elinor, and Selame, Joe. *Developing a Corporate Identity.* New York: Lebhar-Friedman Books, 1980.

Topor, Robert S. *Marketing Cooperative Extension.* Ithaca, NY: Cornell University Media Services, 1982.

Udell, Jon G., and Laczniak, Gene R. *Marketing in an Age of Change.* New York: John Wiley & Sons, 1981.

U.S. Department of Commerce, Bureau of Economic Analysis. *Business Conditions Digest.* Washington, DC: U.S. Government Printing Office, monthly.

Vichas, Robert P. *Complete Handbook of Profitable Marketing Research Techniques.* Englewood Cliffs, NJ: Prentice-Hall, 1982.

West, Christopher. *Marketing on a Small Budget.* New York: John Wiley & Sons, 1975.

About the Author

Robert S. Topor

Robert (Bob) S. Topor is president of Topor & Associates, a marketing communications consulting firm for schools, colleges, and universities and other nonprofit organizations. He received his bachelor's degree in advertising and journalism from Syracuse in 1958 and began working in the field of marketing nonprofit organizations while still an undergraduate. "I began working on marketing higher education," Topor says, "when it was still thought of as a simple, passive editing activity."

Since this undergraduate beginning, Topor has served on the staffs of Syracuse University; the University of Rochester, where he got his graduate degree; Peterson's Guides to Higher Education; Wright State University; and Cornell University. Today Topor serves as director of marketing promotion for the San Diego Hospital Association and the Sharp HealthCare system in San Diego, California. He and his wife Martha live in San Diego with their sons, Mark and Brad.

While at Cornell, Topor wrote a guidebook describing ways to apply marketing ideas for Cornell Cooperative Extension, a nonprofit educational network in New York State. His marketing concepts have been used nationally for state cooperative extension programs through the U.S. Department of Agriculture. He helped plan and appeared in an instructional videotape used to train cooperative extension leaders in applying marketing ideas to their organizations. He has led marketing sessions for many state cooperative extension meetings.

Topor has consulted for many schools, colleges, and universities and has served as adviser to nonprofit organizations in the U.S. and Canada. He has taught marketing at many seminars and workshops for the Council for Advancement and Support of Education (CASE) and other organizations.

In 1987 CASE presented Topor with the Alice L. Beeman Award. Named for CASE's first president, the Beeman Award recognizes significant editorial contributions to a better understanding of institutional advancement. *Your Personal Guide* is the third book by Topor to be published by CASE. His previous books, *Marketing Higher Education: A Practical Guide* and *Institutional Image: How to Define, Improve, Market It,* are both CASE best sellers.

Topor dedicates the efforts of his company to finding ways to help nonprofits compete and thrive. His latest project is a software program that allows the user to develop a computerized marketing plan. "When people ask me why I have remained interested in marketing nonprofit organizations all these years, I tell them it stems from frustration...frustration at seeing how poorly most nonprofits market themselves," says Topor. What does the future hold for marketing nonprofits? Topor responds, "The future is almost unlimited as organizations discover that marketing can be a direct aid to help them accomplish their missions."